wanting to improve their personal and professional lives. This latest book examines a most important topic—self-mastery—which is so relevant to today's world. In a thoroughly readable and practical examination, backed by evidence of the elements that comprise attaining self-mastery, Williams insightfully provides the knowledge and practical suggestions on attaining self-mastery to achieve personal transformation. -- **Mike Webb**, Senior Vice-President and Chief Administrative Officer, Rogers Corporation.

The Journey to Self-Mastery

Unlocking the Secrets to Personal Transformation

Ray Williams

Author of *Virtuous Leadership: The Character Secrets of Great Leaders*

The Journey to Inner Mastery: Unlocking the Secrets to Personal Transformation

by Ray Williams

Published by Aurelias Publishing

Vancouver, B.C.

Includes bibliographical references.

Amazon ISBN: 9798865972280

1. Self-Mastery. 2. Self-Awareness. 3. Emotional Intelligence.
4. Empathy and Compassion. 5. Managing Emotions.
6. Personal Productivity. 7. Building Resilience.
8. Prosocial Behavior. 8. Moral Choices

Dedication

This book is dedicated to my wife and dearest friend, Diane Williams, who showed me the power and importance of building an inner life of goodness, selflessness, and kindness.

Acknowledgments

The making of a book is rarely a singular enterprise, although the author contributes the creative content. Many people have helped. I am grateful to those who have helped me bring *The Journey to Self-Mastery* to fruition.

First and foremost, I acknowledge my wife and best friend Diane Williams, who contributed countless hours editing my manuscript and offering valuable insights for the book.

My gratitude also goes out to Mike Desjardins, a talented and successful CEO of a leading leadership development company, ViRTUS, for writing the Foreword to the book and making many valuable suggestions.

Gratitude also goes out to Stephanie Frank, entrepreneur extraordinaire and best-selling author, for her support, endorsement, and helpful feedback.

Finally, my immense gratitude goes towards my father, Brinley Williams, who, while deceased these many years, still lives in my memory and heart as a man of the finest character who lived the example of self-mastery.

Table Of Contents

Foreword

In today's fast-paced and complex world, individuals are bombarded with personal and psychological challenges that can profoundly impact their well-being and overall quality of life. Emotional trauma, high workloads, financial pressures, and societal expectations can paralyze us, hindering our ability to take risks and pursue meaningful goals. Recognizing and addressing these challenges is vital to fostering emotional well-being, building resilience, and finding fulfillment in life.

Against this backdrop, *The Journey to Inner Mastery: Unlocking the Secrets to Personal Transformation* by Ray Williams emerges as a touchstone. Williams offers more than a roadmap; he invites us on a transformational quest of self-discovery and growth. His life's work has been dedicated to human betterment, fueled by a deep-seated belief in the innate goodness of humanity and an empathetic understanding of those who struggle in their personal journeys.

As someone who has spent decades in the field of leadership development, I see Williams' work as an essential companion for anyone in a leadership role, whether formal or informal. The book aligns remarkably well with the principles of effective leadership that we at ViRTUS advocate—principles rooted in self-mastery, self-awareness, and the capacity for nuanced judgment.

Williams doesn't just theorize; he provides actionable strategies and contemplative practices to practically integrate wisdom into our daily lives. His book covers a gamut of critical themes, from emotional intelligence and empathy to resilience and moral choices. It's a toolkit that not only serves leaders, but anyone committed to personal and professional growth. By developing what Williams calls "practical wisdom," individuals can navigate the complexities of life more effectively, building meaningful relationships and making value-aligned choices.

In sum, *The Journey to Inner Mastery* is not just a book to be read; it's a manual for life. It serves as a compass guiding us through the labyrinth of self-discovery, offering invaluable, research-backed knowledge and practical strategies for cultivating that elusive practical wisdom. The journey toward self-mastery is indeed unique to each of us. I encourage you to approach it with an open heart, a curious mind, and a willingness to embrace the transformative changes that undoubtedly lie ahead.

In a world clamoring for external success and validation, let this book be your guide to mastering the often-overlooked internal landscape. It's an investment in yourself that will pay dividends in every other area of your life.

Mike Desjardins
CEO, ViRTUS, Inc.

Preface

"Know the world in yourself. Never look for yourself in the world, for this would be to project your illusion."

– Ancient Egyptian Proverbs

For the past forty-plus years I have dedicated my life to helping people become their best selves. My passion was driven by a deep belief in the goodness of humanity and empathy and compassion for those who struggle and look for answers in their personal lives and the world.

In the depths of our hearts, we yearn for personal growth and enlightenment. We seek the wisdom that will guide us on our quest to becoming the best versions of ourselves. Yet, amidst the chaos and complexities of life, it can often feel like an elusive quest, an uphill battle strewn with obstacles, disappointment, and uncertainty.

Life is difficult these days. And at the same time, it can be filled with happiness and personal fulfillment. Public polls and surveys have shown us two worlds—one where people are negative, despondent, angry, and fearful about the world and their personal lives, and the other world is filled with altruism, hope, happiness, and fulfilment. In reconciling those two worlds, many people seek ways to make the right choices and decisions and live true to their positive values and beliefs. In short, they seek inner wisdom.

In today's fast-paced and complex world, individuals encounter various personal and psychological challenges that can profoundly affect their well-being and overall quality of life. For example, emotional trauma caused by experiences such as abuse, violence, or significant losses can leave deep scars and disrupt your ability to form healthy relationships or trust others.

Also, the relentless demands of modern life, including high workloads, financial pressures, and societal expectations, contribute to decreased motivation. Whether rooted in past trauma or generated by external events and uncertainties, fear can paralyze individuals and hinder their ability to take risks and pursue their goals. Moreover, navigating through obstacles in various domains of life, such as career, relationships, or personal growth, can be daunting and disheartening, often resulting in a sense of defeat and difficulty in moving forward. Recognizing and addressing these challenges is essential to fostering emotional well-being, building resilience, and finding fulfillment in an increasingly complex world.

Studying how we can act upon our world is not enough. It misses the whole world within us, and true self-mastery lies there.

The essence of this book also lies in its practicality. Each section of the book is imbued with actionable strategies and contemplative practices aimed at helping you integrate wisdom into your daily life. The book is not a mere collection of theories but a roadmap that invites you to roll up your sleeves and embark on a transformational quest of self-discovery and growth.

Self-mastery is about a deep understanding of human nature, an ability to make sound judgments, and the capacity to apply knowledge and values to real-life situations. It involves the skill of making morally and ethically informed decisions that consider the context, consequences, and long-term implications.

Achieving self-mastery requires a combination of experience, critical thinking, empathy, self-reflection, and a commitment to continuous learning. It involves cultivating honesty, integrity, compassion, and humility. By developing practical wisdom, individuals can navigate complex situations effectively, resolve conflicts, build meaningful relationships, and make choices that align with their values. The outcomes of self-mastery include increased personal well-being, enhanced social relationships, the ability to contribute positively to society, and fostering a sense of purpose and fulfilment in life. It is the key to personal transformation.

This book will examine in detail the elements of self-mastery including the art and science of self-reflection, managing your emotional world, enhancing your productivity, dealing with the chaos in the external world, and making moral choices to serve as a north star to guide your life.

This book covers the following themes:

- ☐ Self-awareness.
- ☐ Managing your thoughts and emotions.
- ☐ Emotional intelligence.
- ☐ Empathy and compassion.
- ☐ Resilience.
- ☐ Prosocial behavior.
- ☐ Personal productivity.
- ☐ Moral choices.

The Journey to Self-Mastery has held deep personal meaning for me. For much of my life, not including my dedication to family, and close friends, my focus has been external—on career, accomplishments, financial gain, and activities, --with precious time left over to examine my internal world, what is inside me. Later in life, I realized that was unbalanced, and in recent years, I have spent more time understanding and practicing what it takes for personal mastery—with satisfying results.

I hope this book can be a compass to guide you through the labyrinth of self-discovery, offering invaluable insights, research-backed knowledge, and practical strategies to cultivate that practical wisdom.

Each individual's journey toward self-mastery is unique, and your experiences will shape your course. As you embark upon this journey, remember to approach it with an open heart, a curious mind, and a willingness to embrace the changes that lie ahead.

Whatever path you have chosen in life, or if you are still in the process of discovering what it should be, I hope you embrace your journey with hope, curiosity, and a desire for self-mastery.

Introduction

"He who controls others may be powerful, but he who has mastered himself is mightier still."

– Lao Tzu

What is Self-Mastery?

What comes to mind when you hear the term "self-mastery?" Perhaps you see a martial arts master—always composed, focused, and in charge. You might also see someone in complete control of their destiny and their entire life planned out.

Answer honestly. Do you regularly display these characteristics and feel in control of your personal life, job, and goals? Or do you occasionally feel you have less control over your thoughts, emotions, and behaviors than others?

According to psychological studies, self-mastery—the capacity to comprehend, control, and harness your thoughts, feelings, and behaviors to meet life's obstacles with assurance, insight, and fulfillment—is essential for well-being. Also, self-mastery is associated with lower levels of stress, anxiety, and depression as well as improved general mental health.

Self-mastery entails acquiring a keen sense of self, emotional intelligence, and self-control as well as engaging in moral, virtuous, and ethical behaviors.

Ancient Wisdom

The ancient philosophers and sages saw self-mastery as a pathway to personal growth and enlightenment because it allowed individuals to transcend their base desires, emotions, and external influences. Self-mastery was seen as a transformative process that enabled individuals to live by reason and moral values, leading to a more meaningful and virtuous existence.

The renowned Greek philosopher Socrates emphasized the importance of self-knowledge as the foundation of wisdom. He preached that by understanding ourselves better, we could master a better understanding of the world and make wiser decisions.

Plato, a student of Socrates, expounded upon the concept of self-mastery in his philosophical works. In his dialogue *Phaedrus,* Plato discussed the tripartite divisions of the human soul into reason, emotion, and desire. According to Plato, self-mastery involves harmonizing these different aspects of the self, with reason acting as the guiding force. He saw self-mastery as a prerequisite for achieving wisdom and living a virtuous life.

Aristotle, a student of Plato, regarded self-mastery as an essential component of moral development. In his work, *Nicomachean Ethics* he emphasized the concept of "virtue ethics." He believed that by cultivating virtues, individuals could achieve "eudaimonia," which can be translated as flourishing or a life well-lived. For Aristotle, self-mastery played a crucial role in the pursuit of virtue and the attainment of wisdom.

Epictetus, a Greek Stoic philosopher, focused extensively on the theme of self-mastery. In his work *Enchiridion,* he taught that true freedom and inner tranquility could only be attained by controlling your desires, emotions, and thoughts. Epictetus emphasized the importance of self-discipline, resilience and aligning your actions with reason.

Marcus Aurelius, a Stoic philosopher and Roman Emperor, highlighted the significance of self-mastery in his *Meditations.* He emphasized the need for individuals to control their desires, emotions, and reactions to external events, believing that by mastering themselves, individuals could cultivate inner peace, resilience, and a sense of tranquility. He recognized that self-mastery involved taking responsibility for your own thoughts, emotions, and actions, leading to a deeper understanding of yourself and the world.

Lao Tzu, the ancient Chinese philosopher and founder of Taoism, emphasized the concept of *Wu Wei*, often translated as "effortless action" or "non-doing." Lao Tzu believed that by aligning yourself with the natural flow of the universe and practicing non-attachment, you could achieve self-mastery and wisdom.

Gautama Buddha, a wandering ascetic and religious teacher who lived in the 6th or 5th century BCE in India, founded Buddhism. His teachings revolve around self-mastery to reach enlightenment and liberation from suffering. Buddha emphasized the practice of mindfulness and meditation to develop awareness of your thoughts, emotions, and sensations. By cultivating mindfulness and non-attachment, individuals could overcome attachments and illusions of the ego and gain self-mastery.

Modern Viewpoints

Self-mastery is not limited to ancient times, as modern experts and authors have recognized its importance in personal development. In his hierarchy of needs theory, psychologist Abraham Maslow suggests that self-actualization, the pinnacle of human development, involves self-mastery and realizing your full potential.

In his book, *The 7 Habits of Highly Effective People*, Stephen R. Covey emphasizes the need for self-mastery through the development of proactive habits and principles. In his book, *The Power of Now*, a popular modern author, Eckhart Tolle, emphasized the importance of mastering your thoughts and living in the present moment as a path to enlightenment.

Google's *Search Inside Yourself* program focuses on cultivating emotional intelligence and self-mastery among employees, aiming to enhance self-awareness, emotion regulation, empathy and interpersonal skills, contributing to employee well-being and effectiveness in the workplace.

The Elements of Self-Mastery

The following can be considered elements of self-mastery:

- **Emotional intelligence.** Self-mastery is closely tied to emotional intelligence, which has been recognized as crucial for success in various domains.

- **Resilience.** Self-mastery is enhanced and strengthened when we effectively deal with adversity and mental and emotional challenges to develop greater resilience.

- **Compassion and Empathy.** Attaining self-mastery is complete if we exhibit our capacity to show empathy and compassion to others and to ourselves.

- **Emotion regulation.** Exercising self-control and managing emotions effectively contributes to greater well-being, positive relationships, and personal productivity.

- **Personal productivity.** Self-mastery is strengthened when we effectively develop and institute personal and professional productivity strategies.

- **Self-Awareness.** Developing greater self-awareness, including self-reflection and mindfulness, enhances our capacity for self-mastery.

- **Proactive social behavior.** Beliefs, attitudes, and behavior such as empathy, compassion, kindness, and altruism strengthen self-mastery.

- **Moral choices.** Developing beliefs and behaviors grounded in a strong sense of morality, ethics and virtue supports and strengthens an individual's capacity for self-mastery.

The Benefits of Self-Mastery

Self-Mastery accrues many benefits for you. It can:

- ☐ Help to control your emotional impulses.

- ☐ Assist in achieving clarity on what is essential and what is not.

- ☐ Help in making decisions based on rational thinking.

- ☐ Help take control of your life.

- ☐ Give the necessary nudges to follow through with your intentions and promises.

- ☐ Help develop attitudes, beliefs, and habits so that you can lead your life to the fullest.

- ☐ Help you find happiness and fulfillment.

- ☐ Help you live in the present moment.

- ☐ Help you regulate emotion and accept negative thoughts and emotions as valid and useful.

- ☐ Help you create room for good feelings like happiness, fulfilment, gratitude, and love.

- ☐ Help you develop and maintain curiosity and commitment to ongoing learning.

Summary and Follow-Up

Self-mastery begins from the inside out. We cannot master our external lives if we are not masters of ourselves. Engaging in a systematic effort to achieve self-mastery is the secret to personal growth and fulfillment. Appendix A contains strategies for attaining self-mastery.

1

Self-Awareness

"Man know thyself; then thou shalt know the Universe and God."

– Pythagoras

Some Questions to Consider

1. What is your definition of self-awareness?

2. Why is self-awareness a foundation for achieving self-mastery?

3. What are the activities or behaviors you have engaged in to enhance your level of self-awareness?

4. Are you conscious of your thoughts and emotions as you are experiencing them?

5. How does self-awareness contribute positively to developing your strengths and character?

6. Does your awareness of your "self" align with how others perceive you?

7. How do you make time and effort to engage in self-reflection.?

Understanding Ourselves: A Journey Through Time

Ever wondered why some people seem to know exactly who they are, while others are still figuring it out? Self-awareness is the secret. It's like having a mirror for your mind, helping you understand your feelings, beliefs, strengths, and weaknesses. It's not about constantly looking at yourself, but about deep understanding who you are.

Self-awareness enables you to reflect upon your experience, evaluate your actions in relationship to your values and goals, and make deliberate choices based on this understanding.

While self-awareness is central to who you are, it is not something you are acutely focused on at every moment of every day. Instead, self-awareness becomes woven into the fabric of who you are and emerges at different points depending on the situation and your personality.

We aren't born with a full understanding of ourselves. Babies start to get a basic sense of who they are at around a year old. By the time they are 18 months old, they have a stronger sense of identity.

According to researchers, self-consciousness can be an aspect of self-awareness. You become self-conscious when you focus and identify elements of your internal self—beliefs, values, purpose, and emotions. Some researchers say self-awareness is like a muscle—the more you use it, the better you understand yourself.

So why is this important? Knowing yourself helps you make better choices, achieve your goals, and master your thoughts and emotions. It is the foundation for self-mastery.

Self-Awareness Through the Ages

Although it is occasionally suggested that our focus on self-awareness is a peculiarly modern phenomenon, originating with the French mathematician Descartes ("I think, therefore I am"), it is the topic of lively ancient and medieval debates and writings.

As I read about the wisdom of ancient philosophers and leaders, I was struck by their almost universal belief about the importance of self-knowledge and self-awareness as the foundation for proper action and behavior and, thereby, self-mastery.

The phrase *"nosce te ipsum,"* or *"know thyself"* has been an ageless theme throughout history, reflected in the writings of great thinkers such as Socrates, Ovid, and Cicero, and in the sayings of the Seven Sages of

Greece; in early Christian writings, as well as in Vedic literature, and in Taoist texts.

Legends tell us that the seven sages of ancient Greece who laid the foundation for Western culture gathered in Delphi and encapsulated their wisdom into this expression. It was subsequently attributed to a dozen other authors, of which Thales of Miletus most commonly takes the honor.

The ancient Greek playwright Aeschylus used the maxim "know thyself" in his play *Prometheus Bound,* in which Prometheus bemoans the injustice of having been bound to a cliffside by Zeus, king of the Olympian gods. The demi-god Oceanus visits Prometheus and admonishes him to "know thyself" before he blames others.

Socrates' student Plato expressed the idea of "Know Thyself" extensively through the words of Socrates. In Plato's *Charmides*, and *Protagoras*, Socrates engages in a long dialogue about how we may gain knowledge of ourselves. In Plato's *Philebus* dialogue, Socrates refers to the same usage of "know thyself" to build an example of the ridiculous for the character in the dialogue, *Protarchus.* Socrates says in *Phaedrus*, that people make themselves appear ridiculous when they are trying to know obscure things before they know themselves.

In Socrates' voice, Plato also argues that understanding yourself enables one to understand others. In Plato's Socratic dialogue *Apology,* Socrates declares that "the unexamined life is not worth living," and that wisdom is only attainable through solitary introspection without the influence of others.

The Stoic philosophers discussed and wrote extensively about the self-examined life. Their recipe for evolving self-awareness included being suspicious about your own perceptions and opinions of events until they were tested, and secondly, taking an opposite approach to evaluate the behavior of others--for example, being sympathetic before being suspicious.

Despite the commonly held belief that the idea of self-awareness originated with the Greeks, it may have originated from other ancient cultures. Evidence exists, for example, from the Coffin Texts of ancient Egypt in 2000 B.C. Other evidence shows an even earlier origin, back to 3000 B.C., from the Old Kingdom Egyptian dynasties, which would predate the Hindu Vedas, the Greek philosophers, and the Chinese I-Ching. Hindu scriptures focus on self-awareness as a way of attaining immortality. The Hindu Upanishads argue man is not born with self-awareness, so it becomes a lifelong challenge.

The Platonic tradition continued through the influence of St. Augustine and is associated with the view that the mind "gains the knowledge of [itself] through itself." Thus, self-awareness requires no awareness of the external world. St. Thomas Aquinas, writing in the thirteenth century, synthesized Platonic and Aristotelian thought by claiming that there is a form of self-awareness--awareness that one exists--for which, "the mere presence of the mind suffices."

In 1651, the 17th-century English philosopher Thomas Hobbes used the term *nosce te ipsum* which he translated as "read thyself" in his famous work, *The Leviathan*. He asserted that one learns more by studying oneself, particularly the feelings that influence thoughts and motivate actions. In 1734, English poet Alexander Pope's poem "An Essay on Man, Epistle II", expresses the concept in the lines "Know then thyself, presume not God to scan, the proper study of mankind is Man." In 1750, American political leader Benjamin Franklin's *Poor Richard's Almanac* claimed, "There are three Things extremely hard, Steel, a Diamond, and to know yourself." In 1754, French philosopher Jean-Jacques Rousseau in his *Discourse on the Origin of Inequality*, emphasized the importance of the inscription of the Temple at Delphi.

In 1831, American literary great Ralph Waldo Emerson wrote a poem entitled "Know Thyself" which focused on knowing the "God" within each person. In 1832, English writer Samuel T. Coleridge wrote a poem entitled "Self Knowledge" in which the text centers on the Delphic maxim "Know Thyself."

"Know Thyself" has subsequently appeared in many literary works, from Shakespearian theatre and Sufi literature. The concept of self-awareness also appeared in the eighteenth century with American poet Walt Whitman.

In more recent times in the movie medium, the moviemakers Wachowski brothers used another Latin version of "know thyself" *nosce te ipsum* as an inscription over the Oracle's door in their movies *The Matrix* and *The Matrix Revolutions*. The transgender character Nomi in the Netflix show *Sense8*, also directed by the Wachowskis, has a tattoo on her arm with the Greek version of the phrase. "Know Thyself."

A. Self-Awareness and Values

What are the principles or values that you live your life by? What do you stand for? What are you willing to sacrifice or even die for? Your values can define the answer to those questions.

Think of values as your internal GPS. They guide your choices and determine what's right or meaningful for you. Values can be things such as honesty, family, compassion, or service.

Understanding your values is a two-step process. First, you need to get crystal clear about what really matters to you. Then, you must show those values to the world through your words and actions.

What Does Self-Awareness Research Tell Us?

Lately, there's been a resurgence in studying self-awareness, especially when it comes to leadership. It seems that leaders who lack self-awareness often get themselves into difficulties.

Some researchers, like neuroscientist V.S. Ramahandran, believe our brains play a big part in self-awareness. He suggests that certain brain cells—mirror neurons—can help us understand others and ourselves better. He says, "These neurons can not only help simulate other people's behavior but can be turned inward."

Researchers Shelley Duval and Robert Wicklund, authors of their influential book *A Theory of Objective Self-Awareness*, contend that when we focus on ourselves, we end up comparing our actions to our values, making us extra aware of our behavior.

The study conducted by Julia Carden and colleagues Rebecca J. Jones and Jonathan Passmore, in their article in the *Journal of Management Education*, argue the following:

- ☐ Self-aware people make better choices and are better team members and leaders.

- ☐ Self-aware people are more considerate of others.

- ☐ Self-awareness is both external and internal.

- ☐ People can develop their self-awareness through reflecting and learning from others.

- ☐ High self-awareness, claimed to lead to better decision-making, is linked to team performance and authentic leadership.

- ☐ People with high levels of self-awareness are more likely to be promoted and are more effective leaders.

- ☐ A Stanford Business School Business Advisory Council survey rated self-awareness as the most important trait leaders require.

- ☐ Self-awareness is both conscious and unconscious.

- ☐ Self-awareness is also related to being sensitive to the feelings of others, and your impact on others.

- ☐ Self-awareness is connected to self-efficacy and emotional intelligence, both of which are viewed as a route to increased leadership effectiveness.

The Seven Pillars of Self-Awareness

An examination of the research literature can summarize the following components of Self-Awareness:

1. **Beliefs and values.** Your core beliefs and things you cherish. They shape how you react and behave.

2. **Mental state.** How you think and feel. Emotions shape feelings, and sometimes, you must be hyper-aware of your thoughts.

3. **Body talk.** How your body reacts, like a sudden adrenaline rush or muscle tightening.

4. **Who you are.** Recognizing your personality traits, strengths, and areas for growth.

5. **Why you do what you do.** Your inner drives and reasons behind your actions.

6. **Actions speak louder.** The behaviors that others notice.

7. **Mirror, mirror.** How others see you is sometimes best understood through their feedback.

Understanding Self-Efficacy and Self-Awareness

Our belief in our ability to succeed, often called "self-efficacy," sets the stage for thinking, behaving, and feeling. People with strong self-efficacy know their flaws and abilities and choose to utilize these qualities to the best of their ability. People who lack self-efficacy can evade challenges and quickly feel discouraged by setbacks partly because they are not self-aware and therefore, often do not change their attitude.

According to researcher Matthew Lippincott, in his research he argues: "Developing emotional self-awareness is a crucial first step in effective leadership because it lays the foundation upon which the other eleven Emotional and Social Intelligence Competencies are built. We can't develop skills like emotional self-control, empathy, or collaboration unless we come from a place of emotional self-awareness."

Self-aware people recognize their limitations and strengths and welcome constructive feedback from others. In contrast, people with low self-awareness may respond to critical feedback as a threat or sign of failure.

It's clear that self-awareness is foundational to emotional intelligence and is critical to our ability to communicate effectively with and build relationships of trust with others. Self-aware individuals are skilled at self-monitoring and adapting their behaviors to relate effectively with others.

The Journey Inward: Getting to Know Yourself

Ever wondered why some people have an "inner voice" that guides them? Lars Hall, a cognitive scientist, suggests that it's because of the ability for introspection. It's like deeply diving into your mind and understanding your beliefs, values, and motivations. This insight then helps shape your decisions and actions. Paying attention to your emotions as they happen is essential. Imagine your mind is like a busy highway. Every thought is a car. Instead of getting lost in the traffic, step back and observe. This practice helps make more thoughtful choices instead of just reacting impulsively.

Usually, when we have "a thought," we engage with it automatically, fusing with it (i.e., we think the thought is who we are). But remember, thoughts are not facts but biochemical activity in our brains. As we know, some thoughts can be very sticky, making it difficult to step back. With mindfulness, we practice gently pulling away from thoughts, again and again, pausing, observing, and creating more and more space between the "mental event" and the response.

Each time we practice noticing and labelling our thoughts, we rewire the brain because we are doing something different than what we normally do. Each time we notice and label, we disengage from the default mode network, "a system of connected brain areas that show increased activity when a person is not focused on the outside world." Instead of automatically engaging with the thought, we are stepping out of thought, creating a space, allowing for choosing and responding rather than reacting and becoming the wise observer of our mind. In this way, we are less at the mercy of our default mode, which can get stuck in unhelpful rumination and preoccupation. When we become more aware, we wake up, free ourselves from our conditioning, and begin to live more consciously and intentionally.

Neuroscience research has shown that the labelling of thought helps to regulate emotion and promote insight during times of stress and emotional upset. Labelling with kindness is very beneficial as it slows the thinking mind, creating a space to step back and observe. This also has the effect of calming the stress reaction in our body and not getting caught in the intensity of the emotion.

Research has also shown that mental noticing and labelling produce a relaxing effect in our body, which helps us detach from thoughts. We stop identifying so personally with our thoughts and reacting emotionally to them. Rather than getting caught up in our thoughts, we train our minds to notice and label. Then, we have more choices regarding which thoughts to pay attention to intentionally. By de-emphasizing rumination or emotion with our attention through noting and labelling, we can free ourselves from excessive preoccupation or reactivity, becoming calmer and turning to the good things in our lives.

The External Mirror: How Others See Us

Self-awareness isn't just about looking inward and understanding how others perceive us. It's like having a mirror that reflects on how our actions and words affect those around us.

However, it's not always easy. Richard Boyatzis and Annie McKee, co-authors with Daniel Goleman of the book *Primal Leadership,* note that stress can cloud our self-perception and how we read others. We can miss important cues that would help us interact with others.

Why Self-Awareness is a Challenge

1. Blindspots. Ever wonder why sometimes you don't see things that are obvious to others? Blindspots can mislead even the best of us into bad or unethical choices, even when we believe we're doing the right thing.

In the book by Ann E. Tenbrunsel and Max H. Bazerman *Blind Spots: Why We Fail to Do What's Right and What to Do About It,* they argue *that good people do bad things without knowing* they are doing anything wrong. This can also create motivational blindness, which is the tendency not to notice the unethical actions of others or us when it is against our own best interests to notice. Blind spots can also create and reinforce the "dark triad" or Machiavellian part of us that behaves according to self-interest and, often, without regard for moral principles.

In his book *Leadership Blindspots: How Successful Leaders Identify and Overcome the Weaknesses That Matter,* Robert Bruce Shaw describes the 20 most common blind spots he has seen while working as an executive coach for hundreds of professionals. Potential and current leaders would benefit from reviewing their list.

I found some commonalities in reviewing Shaw's leader blindspots and comparing them to my experience in working with C-Suite executives for the last three decades. They:

☐ Overestimate their capabilities (overconfidence).

☐ Want to be right rather than effective (ego).

☐ Believe the rules (including ethics) don't apply to them (entitlement).

☐ Put personal ambition and interests before the interests of employees and the organization (self-interest and narcissism).

☐ Are oblivious to the negative impact on others (low emotional intelligence).

2. Defence Mechanisms. Our minds have built-in shields that sometimes prevent us from seeing the truth about ourselves. These are like protective walls, keeping painful truths at bay. But they can also keep us from growing. Researchers Cam Caldwell and Linda Hayes explain how defence mechanisms such as projection, displacement, undoing, isolation, sublimation, and denial are virtually universal phenomena and can lead to feedback-avoiding behavior. Other researchers suggest that anticipating a desired conclusion and viewing the world through a self-serving bias can directly affect how people gather evidence and reach conclusions about themselves.

3. Self-Deception. Think of this as a little voice that whispers comforting lies inside your head. However, it can distort our view of reality. It's like wearing glasses with the wrong prescription. Self-deception is one of many defence mechanisms that enable us to maintain self-esteem and our identity. In writing about self-deception as a coping mechanism, Daniel Goleman explained that self-deception was often a subconscious effort to avoid pain and anxiety, skewing our conscious awareness by filtering out painful information. Psychiatrist Scott Peck, author of *The Road Less Travelled*, noted that frequently, those who deceive others or themselves do so unwittingly and often without a conscious awareness of their motives for their deceptions. In writing about the dissonance of self-deception, Richard Boyatzis, Daniel Goleman, and Annie McKee describe it in their book *Primal Leadership* as follows:: "We end up seeing the world in very black-and-white terms, and we slowly lose the ability to see ourselves, or those around us, realistically. We miss a lot. Then, when things do go wrong, it is very easy to continue to blame others, and feel sorry for us as things deteriorate--especially when the downturn feels like a surprise and follows a period of denial."

Another reason we can deceive ourselves about reality and are not aware is that we are "not present" a good part of the time, but rather, our minds are in the past or the future. Another way of saying this is that a person is not mindful.

B. Self-Assessment Inaccuracies

A common approach to raising self-awareness is self-reporting assessments, which are more prevalent than 360-degree assessments, which involve the assessment by others. Recent research shows that self-assessments need to be more accurate.

In a study of more than 13,000 professionals, researchers found almost no relationship between self-assessment and objective performance ratings. A second study by these researchers found more than 33% of engineers rated their performance in the top 5% relative to peers. Another study showed that 94% of college professors thought they were above average in their jobs. This is often called the Dunning–Kruger effect, in which people with limited competence in a particular domain overestimate their abilities.

How Self-Esteem Has Damaged Self-Awareness

Accurate self-awareness and self-assessment become far more difficult if we have a distorted or exaggerated view of ourselves. Some experts blame this development on the self-esteem movement of the last few decades.

Self-esteem can be defined as an individual's subjective evaluation of their own worth. Social psychologists and co-authors of *Social Psychology* (4*th* *Edition*) Eliot Smith and Diane Mackie have defined it: "The self-concept is what we think about the self; self-esteem is the positive or negative evaluations of the self, as in how we feel about it."

These days, self-esteem has acquired a second meaning: "an unduly high opinion of yourself; vanity." According to Jean M. Twenge, professor of psychology at San Diego State University, this definition best fits Generation Y. She argues that inflated egos leave many young people with unrealistic expectations, and their inability to achieve these can lead to depression. She says it is no coincidence that the U.S. Center for Disease Control and Prevention in Atlanta, Georgia, reported that one in nine Americans over 12 now takes antidepressants -a quadrupling of the rate since the late 1980s.

Twenge sees another sign of dangerously overblown self-esteem in rising levels of narcissism. She found that twice as many college students had high levels of narcissism in 2006 compared with the early 1980s. Narcissists tend to be intolerant of criticism and prone to cheating and aggression. "These are the people who wind up arguing over a grade in your office," she says. In her book, *The Narcissism Epidemic*, written by co-author W. Keith Campbell, she recounts anecdotes of hiring fake paparazzi to make themselves look famous and buying "McMansions" on credit as evidence of the Americans' overblown ego.

"We have taken individualism too far," says Twenge, and popular culture reflects this. She has worked with University of Kentucky social psychologist Nathan DeWall and others to chart an increase in the frequency of the word "I" in the lyrics of hit U.S. pop songs from 1980 to 2007.

Twenge blames four factors: Changes in parenting styles, the cult of celebrity, the internet and easy credit. "All of these things allow people to have an inflated sense of self in which the appearance of performance is more important than the actual performance," she says.

Organizational psychologist Tasha Eurich argues persuasively that we are "living in an age of focus on self and self-aggrandizement." This corresponds to the rise of the age of self-esteem. Eurich goes on to say, "An excessive self–focus obscures our vision of those around us and distorts our ability to see ourselves as we really are." She quotes the research that shows an inverse relationship between how special we think we are and how self-aware we are.

What's interesting about this trend in self-focus is that it is relevant to the theme of this book. The self-focus is not internal through practices such as reflection and self-awareness; it is external in which individuals compare and measure themselves against others.

Psychologist Roy Baumeister has studied the issue of self-esteem extensively. He reviewed 15,000 studies and found:

☐ The relationship between self-esteem and success was virtually nonexistent.

☐ People with high self-esteem are more violent and aggressive and more likely to have relationship problems.

The Benefits of Enhanced Self-Awareness

Self-awareness is now seen as a constructive concept in psychology. Humans viewing themselves merely as objects can have detrimental psychological effects on overall well-being. Several psychologists and researchers have zeroed in on self-awareness to determine what it is, the impact and benefits, and the impact and outcomes for others.

According to researcher Kristin Neff, the key to self-awareness is the inclusion of objective and subjective states and the practice of self-compassion.

A study by Anna Sutton published in *Europe's Journal of Psychology* found that enhanced self-awareness improved self-acceptance, self-confidence, proactivity, and stress reduction. A 2015 study by Sutton and colleagues found self-awareness training for employees was associated with improved job satisfaction, greater appreciation of diversity, increased confidence, better communication, and general well-being.

Research by Richard Boyatzis and colleagues has shown that self-aware leaders are more effective in inspiring and motivating others, building strong relationships, and adapting their leadership styles to different situations. The researchers also found that leaders with greater self-awareness were more receptive to feedback and creating a positive and inclusive work environment.

Tasha Eurich has spent more than 10 years surveying people about their levels of self-awareness. She found that while 95% of study participants think they're self-aware, only about 10% to 15% are self-aware.

"Self-awareness allows us to shift perspective, to see both hard realities and possibilities," explains Eurich. "We've found that people who are more self-aware are also more self-accepting." Eurich, also an executive coach, tells her clients that moving bravely into self-awareness can help them feel empowered as they begin to see themselves and their impact more clearly.

In an article in *Harvard Business Review,* Eurich said "Research suggests that when we see ourselves clearly, we are more confident and more creative. We make sounder decisions, build stronger relationships, and communicate more effectively. We're less likely to lie, cheat, and steal. We are better workers who get more promotions. And we're more effective leaders with more satisfied employees and more profitable companies."

The Case for Self-Reflection

Self-reflection can be defined as "serious thought about your character and actions," "the activity of thinking about your feelings and behavior, and the reasons that may lie behind them," and "the examination or observation of your own mental and emotional processes."

Reflective thinking is important because the world is unpredictable, and new or unexpected events occur. During reflective thinking, we pause to examine the consequences of various actions and events, and it helps us make decisions.

Reflective skills harness our prefrontal brain's capacity for executive attention, prosocial behavior, empathy, and self-regulation. As we reflect on our own internal states, the resonance circuitry that evolved to connect with others' minds is primed to sense the deep nature of our own intentional world.

Management expert Margaret J. Wheatley has said, "Without reflection, we go blindly on our way, creating more unintended consequences, and failing to achieve anything useful."

Jack Mezirow, in his book, *Fostering Critical Reflection in Adulthood: A Guide to Transformative and Emancipatory Learning,* describes critical reflection as "a type of reflection characterized by an individual's re-examination of the presuppositions that inform their own beliefs, thoughts, and actions."

Learning occurs both by doing and by thinking about what we do. Often, we go through our day-to-day life without spending too much time thinking about our experiences. Reflection is a tool to keep your thoughts and actions running through the active part of your brain before it gets to the reactive part of your brain.

At its simplest, reflection is about careful thought. But the kind of reflection that involves the conscious consideration and analysis of beliefs and actions for the purpose of learning. Reflection gives the brain an opportunity to pause amid the chaos, untangle and sort through observations and experiences, consider multiple possible interpretations, and create meaning.

Few companies give their employees reflection time. The focus instead is on productivity and "working harder" to meet deadlines and beat the competition. Yet, new research demonstrates the value of reflection in helping people do a better job. In an article in *Harvard Business Review,* Francesca Gino and Gary Pisano of Harvard Business School, Giada Di Stefano of HEC Paris, and Bradley Staats of the University of North Carolina show that "reflecting on what you've done teaches you to do it better next time." Further, they find that the effect of reflection on learning is mediated by a greater perceived ability to achieve a goal (i.e., self-efficacy).

Self-reflection as a method of enhancing self-awareness can have measurable productivity benefits in organizations. The researchers demonstrated that employees who spent 15 minutes at the end of the day reflecting on their work performed 23% better after only 10 days than those who did not reflect.

According to the former director of the Accenture Institute of Strategic Change and coauthor of the book *The Attention Economy: Understanding the New Currency of Business,* Tom Davenport: "Understanding and managing attention is now the single most important determinant of business success," adding that self-reflection is a critical component of developing your attention.

Self-reflection can come in many forms, including meditation. LinkedIn CEO Jeff Weiner, Oprah Winfrey, and even Jerry Seinfeld have all credited some form of meditation to their success. Weiner believes it helps him develop empathy and compassion, while Oprah feels it enriches her faith. Either way, studies show that self-reflection, be it meditation or otherwise, is a powerful method to reduce stress and enable people in leadership positions to make better decisions.

Jennifer Porter, a contributor to *the Harvard Business Review* states, "The most useful reflection involves the conscious consideration and analysis of beliefs and actions for learning." Reflection enables leaders to create meaning from their experiences. "Meaning becomes learning, which can then inform future mindsets and actions. For leaders, this 'meaning-making' is crucial to their ongoing growth and development", Porter writes.

Self-reflection and the subsequent self-awareness born from the practice encourage leaders to step back and consider how their leadership affects the organization and the teams and people they work with.

Author Kevin Cashman writes in *The Pause Principle,* "The transition is one from expertise and control to authenticity and shared purpose. This crucial evolution requires a sufficient, intentional pause to build self-awareness, foster team collaboration, and increase strategic innovation. Pause is a catalytic process that has the potential to bring forth transformative shifts if practiced consciously."

In my book *I Know Myself and Neither Do You: Why Charisma, Confidence and Pedigree Won't Take You Where You Want to Go,* I thoroughly examine how self-reflection can increase leaders' self-awareness and make them better leaders.

I argue that "Reflective thinking is important because the world is unpredictable, and new or unexpected events occur. During reflective thinking, we pause to examine the consequences of various actions and events, and it helps us make decisions. Reflective skills harness our prefrontal capacity for executive attention, prosocial behavior, empathy, and self-regulation. As we reflect on our internal states, the resonance circuitry that evolved to connect with others' minds is primed to sense the deep nature of our intentional world."

Mindfulness

"Would you like to save the world from the degradation and destruction it seems destined for? Then quietly go to work on your own self-awareness. If you want to awaken all of humanity, then awaken all of yourself. If you want to eliminate the suffering in the world, then eliminate all that is dark and negative in yourself. Truly, the greatest gift you have to give is that of your own self-transformation."

- Lao Tzu

Daniel J. Siegel, author of *The Mindful Brain*, believes that by diving deep into our experiences, we better understand our thoughts and emotions. In his words, being "aware of our awareness" is a transformative experience.

What is mindfulness? At its core, it's about being present. It's about paying attention to the moment without any judgment. It's noticing the world around you, your feelings and emotions and thoughts, just as they are.

Definitions of mindfulness describe a psychological trait, a practice of cultivating mindfulness meditation, a mode or state of awareness, or a psychological process. Another definition of mindfulness is the awareness that arises through "paying attention in a particular way, on purpose, in the present moment, and nonjudgmentally."

Researchers emphasize the role of focused attention in mindfulness, suggesting that it involves two main parts:

1. Directing our attention purposefully.

2. Reflecting on our external and internal experiences without judgment.

Now, what does this mean for you? In a study titled "The Mindful Self," published in *The Frontiers of Psychology*, Xiao Qianguo and colleagues found that mindfulness leads to positive self-views, like acceptance and compassion. By practicing mindfulness, the authors contend you can see yourself in a clearer light.

These findings suggest that mindfulness practices moderate implicit self-concepts and perspectives on the self and develop positive self-functions with a shift toward healthier personalities.

Being Versus Doing as an Expression of Self-Awareness

In our fast-paced world, we often find ourselves in a "Doing" mode particularly in workplaces. We constantly set goals, plan, complete tasks, and check boxes. But Oxford University psychologist Mark Williams suggests another mode: "Being." This mode is about being present, allowing things to be as they are.

Every day in everything you do, your mind switches between doing mode and being mode. Both are required for healthy living. Here's the difference between the two modes of mind:

Doing	Being
You are aware of how things are and how they should be.	You acknowledge and allow things to be as they are.
You set goals to fix or doing things.	You are open to pleasant, unpleasant, and neutral emotions without judgment.
You exert more effort to achieve	You are open to pleasant,

goals.	unpleasant, and neutral emotions without judgment.
Most of your actions occur automatically without conscious awareness	You have an inner sense of awareness, allowing peace, stillness, and silence.
Your mind is mostly in the past or future, not the present.	You are connected to the present moment.
Your random focus more on things that need fixing or what's missing.	You are very focused and attentive intentionally.
You try to accomplish too many things.	You avoid multi-tasking.
You are not conscious of how your body is feeling at any moment.	You take time to reflect on both your outer and inner experiences.

Summary and Follow-Up

In summary, self-awareness involves recognizing and understanding your own thoughts, emotions, and behaviors. Psychologists, experts, and writers have explored self-awareness from various perspectives, highlighting its importance for personal growth and well-being. Positive self-awareness brings numerous benefits, including improved self-regulation, self-acceptance, decision-making, and interpersonal relationships.

Appendix B contains a self-awareness self-assessment.

2

Managing Your Thoughts and Emotions

"Our feelings are not there to be cast out or conquered. They are there to be engaged and expressed with imagination and intelligence."

– T.K. Coleman

Some Questions to Consider

1. Are you aware in the present moment of your thoughts and emotions as you experience them?

2. Do you take time to reflect on your thoughts and emotions as to what they are trying to tell you?

3. Do you consider negative thoughts and emotions something you shouldn't have?

4. Do you try to suppress or avoid negative thoughts and emotions? What do you do?

5. What do you think is the purpose of having negative thoughts and emotions?

6. Do you believe you should try to always be happy and positive?

7. What are the consequences of you experiencing negative thoughts or emotions?

What are the Differences Between Thoughts and Emotions?

Sometimes it can be difficult to tell thoughts and emotions apart. Some people are better at identifying their thoughts, while others are better at identifying their emotions.

Here are a few strategies to help you distinguish thoughts from emotions:

- ☐ Emotions generally take one word to describe, while thoughts are usually a string of words.

- ☐ Emotions cause feelings all over our body, while thoughts we typically experience only in our head/mind.

- ☐ Thoughts can be fact-checked. We can argue with thoughts, but we can't argue with an emotion. If you can refute or argue with what you are saying, it is probably a thought.

This table of examples can also help you identify the relationship between your emotions and thoughts.

Emotion	Types of Thoughts that Lead to this Emotion	Example of a Connecting Emotion
Shame; Depression	Thoughts of a loss, rejection, or failure.	"They don't like me." "I'll" never be good enough."
Guilt; Shame	Thoughts that you have filed to live up to certain standards: yours', someone else's, or your culture's. Guilt results from self-condemnation and shame fear of the reaction of others.	"I shouldn't have done that." " I should have...." "I'm not what my family wants."
Anger; Irritation; Annoyance	You believe that someone is treating you unfairly or trying to take advantage of you. You make assumptions about	"They shouldn't do that." "Nobody has any manners."

		the intentions of others.	
Frustration	Thoughts that life is not meeting your expectations and should be different.	"Why does traffic always slow down when I'm in a hurry?" "He should have been on time." "I shouldn't have said that."
Anxiety; Worry; Fear; Panic	Thoughts that you are in danger because something bad is going to happen. Negative predictions about the future.	"What if my mind goes blank?" "They're not going to like me." "What if I'm sick?"
Inferiority; Inadequacy	Thinking about how you compare to someone else.	"There's nothing special about me." "All the guys like her, and nobody likes me."
Hopelessness: Discouragement	Thoughts that your problems are indefinite, and things will never get better.	"I'll never find a good job." "I'll be alone forever."

Mastering Your Mind: A Guide to Inner Balance

In life, we often find ourselves swept away by external events, trying to find joy and purpose through material means and outer experiences. But what if the key to true fulfillment and contentment lies within? We can more clearly assess reality, make wiser choices, and advance our capacity for achieving our objectives. As a result, we have more freedom and can live more purposefully.

Our Two Minds

We have two different thinking systems, roughly speaking, which involve different areas of our brains. The behavioral economist and Nobel laureate Daniel Kahneman in his book, *Thinking, Fast and Slow*, refers to them as "System 1" and "System 2," which "respectively produce fast and slow thinking or intuitive (and unconscious) thought and deliberate (and conscious) thought. System 1 operates automatically and quickly, with little effort and no sense of voluntary control. System 2 allocates attention to the effortful mental activities that demand it, including complex computations, often associated with the subjective experience of agency, choice, and concentration.

The autopilot System 1 is our feelings, emotions and instincts. Most of its cognitive functions are performed in the amygdala and other early-evolving brain regions. The freeze, fight, or flight stress response is part of this system, which directs our daily routines, supports quick judgments, and reacts immediately to perilous life-and-death events. The fight-or-flight reaction may have helped us survive in the past, but it is not well suited to contemporary living.

Just as our minds are divided into two thinking systems, our lives are similarly divided between our external environments and our internal thoughts and emotions. While we often focus on the outer world—attracted by entertainment, commerce, and headline-grabbing events—our internal landscape shapes a significant part of our life's experience.

The autopilot system treats a lot of our little pressures, which are not life-threatening, like deadly threats. This results in an unduly stressful experience of daily life, which is detrimental to both mental and physical health. Furthermore, while quick decisions brought on by intuitions and emotions may feel real since they are quick and strong, they can lead us in erroneous actions and harmful results.

The prefrontal cortex, a region of the brain, is at the center of the intentional System 2, which reflects our capacity for rational thought. This way of thinking enables us to manage more difficult mental tasks including managing interpersonal and group interactions, using logic and probabilistic thinking, and picking up new knowledge and ways of behaving and thinking.

The intentional system requires conscious effort to activate, whereas the automatic system doesn't. Fortunately, the deliberate system can activate in circumstances when the autopilot system is prone to make mistakes, especially costly ones, given enough incentive and the right training.

Autopilot (System 1)	Intentional (System 2)
□ Fast, intuitive, emotional self.	□ Conscious reasoning, mindful self.
□ Requires no conscious effort.	□ Takes intentional effort to turn on.
□ Automatic thinking, feeling and behavior habits.	□ Drains mental energy.
□ Makes good decisions most but not all of the time.	□ Use mainly when we learn new information, and when we use reason and logic.
□ Prone to some predictable and systematic errors.	□ Can be trained to turn on when it detects Autopilot System 1 making an error.

Source: Gleb Tsipursky, best-selling author of several books, including *The Truth Seeker's Handbook: A Science-Based Guide*, and *Never Go With Your Gut: How Pioneering Leaders Make the Best Decisions and Avoid Business Disasters*.

A. Dealing with Negative Emotions

Feeling anxious? It might mean you're unprepared (unless you have a general anxiety disorder). Angry? Maybe a boundary has been crossed. By understanding and accepting all our emotions, we can harness their power for good.

Most of us choose to concentrate on the outside world because it significantly impacts our interior world. However, many of our lives in this world occur inwardly, in our bodies and brains. Particularly, our thoughts and feelings can influence the quality of our life.

Although we may think we have control over our lives because we can influence or manipulate the outside environment, actual control over our interior environment is more important and has more lasting effects.

The capacity to govern and control our thoughts, emotions, and behaviors in accordance with our ideas, values, and deeds is a prerequisite for self-mastery.

Every Emotion Has a Purpose

The assertion that there are no useless or "bad" emotions may surprise you. No matter how it may seem, every emotion has a distinct function and important purpose. Authors and researchers Todd Kashdan and Robert Biswas-Diener explore the idea that finding pleasure doesn't include blocking out bad feelings but rather accepting all emotions and learning to use them productively in their insightful book *The Upside of Your Dark Side*. The problem is not with the emotion itself, but with how we react to it, which can either advance us or hinder us.

According to neuropsychologist Rick Hanson, who founded the Wellspring Institute for Neuroscience and Contemplative Wisdom and wrote the *New York Times* bestseller *Buddha's Brain*, people are naturally predisposed to see the negative side. He claims that humans tend to focus on the bad and ignore the good. For our ancestors, avoiding dangers was considerably more crucial than obtaining positive benefits. He beautifully puts it: "Our brains act like Velcro for negative experiences and Teflon for positive ones."

According to Hanson, the amygdala, the limbic system's alarm system, devotes around two-thirds of its neurons to keeping watch for impending negative news or dangerous occurrences. Once set off, this alarm swiftly records unpleasant experiences in memory. Positive experiences, on the other hand, often need more work and time to transition from short-term memory buffers into long-term storage.

Debunking Myths Regarding Emotions

It's important to dispel some popular misconceptions regarding emotions. These "myths" do a disservice to developing good mental health.

Myth 1: An exact emotion can be used for every circumstance. Truth: Our emotions are dynamic reactions to internal and external events, meaning they are not firmly bound to circumstances and constantly fluctuate. Further, there are degrees and shades of those emotions, which underscores the need for emotional literacy.

Myth 2: Neglecting painful emotions is a good idea. Truth: Avoiding difficult emotions or repressing them makes it harder for us to handle them successfully, which could result in dysfunctional responses.

Myth 3: Expressing emotions shows weakness. Truth: Recognizing and understanding our emotions as they arise can help us express ourselves more healthily, and doing so is by no means a sign of weakness. This is particularly important for men, who tend to suppress their emotions more than women.

Myth 4: Negative emotions are undesirable. Truth: Every emotion, whether it's positive or negative, has a purpose. How we handle these emotions and our response to them counts.

Myth 5: Emotions can happen for no apparent cause. Truth: Emotions are frequently warning signs that we must address a certain area of our lives. They are typical reactions to internal or external occurrences.

Myth 6: Emotions are indisputable facts. Truth: Emotions are not facts. Emotions are temporary mental and physical reactions, not unalterable realities. They only continue if we let them.

Myth 7: Expressing emotions is equivalent to experiencing them. Truth: There are two separate parts of emotions: experience and expression. For instance, anger should not result in violent acts like yelling or smashing doors.

Myth 8: Excessive emotion causes a person to lose control. Truth: Context is important. In contrast to lashing out in fury during a traffic incident, expressing great grief after a loss is good.

Myth 9: Emotions never end. Truth: Unless we intentionally suffer, are in a "mood," repress or ignore our emotions, they are fleeting.

Myth 10: We are powerless over our emotions. Truth: Often, our thoughts about a circumstance trigger our emotions, not that situation itself. We can better control our emotions by learning to read situations in a way that is consistent with our well-being. Remember that managing means controlling, not repressing.

The Negativity Bias

As mentioned before, and emphasized by neuroscientist Rick Hanson, our brains have a negativity bias to protect us from harm.

Human negativity bias has been well-established in research. *The Prospect Theory,* developed by Daniel Kahneman and Amos Tversky examines how people make decisions when faced with inherent hazards The fundamental tenet of *The Prospect Theory* and negativity bias is that people tend to make decisions based on avoiding unpleasant experiences rather than seeking out happy ones. Researchers such as Roy F. Baumister, Ellen Tratslavsky, Kathleen Vohs, and Catrin Finenauer have studied this phenomenon and concluded that bad experiences—or the dread of them—significantly impact people more than pleasant ones do.

According to Paul Rozin and Edward Royzman's research, negativity spreads more easily than positive. Our attitudes are more significantly impacted by bad news than by good news, according to a separate study conducted by John Caciopo. Language analysis has also been used to study this negativity bias, and the results show that the English vocabulary contains more negative emotional words (62%) than positive ones (32%).

Jason Moser and his team demonstrated in their research that worry-prone people frequently worsen their bad feelings, despite their best efforts to think optimistically.

Christopher Nass, a professor at Stanford University and the author of *The Man Who Lied to His Laptop: What Machines Teach Us About Human Relationships,* asserts that we frequently give more weight to criticism than praise because we tend to think that those who voice unfavorable opinions are more educated.

Other Research

Other research has focused on the following areas:

☐ How emotion regulation impacts goal-directed behavior.

☐ The influence of negative beliefs and cognitive distortions on emotion regulation.

☐ The impact of emotion regulation on cognitive abilities.

As demonstrated by a study by Michael Posner and colleagues, our ability to guide and regulate our attention, thoughts, and emotional impulses allows us to suppress automatic or impulsive responses and participate in goal-directed behavior.

Aaron Beck, the creator of cognitive therapy, has stressed the significance of thoughts in shaping our mental and emotional states. Beck's cognitive model postulates that negative ideas often referred to as cognitive distortions, play a role in the emergence and maintenance of emotional distress. According to research conducted by Beck and his associates, cognitive therapy, which focuses on and combats negative beliefs, is beneficial in treating a range of mental health issues.

Richard Lazarus's *Emotion and Adaptation*, argues that emotions have intentionality and that our cognition determines their significance and force. This then makes us judge whether we can cope with the external event or situation, which forms an emotional reaction.

B. Emotion Regulation

We often hear that the key to happiness is to ignore or push away negative thoughts and emotions. However, research suggests that accepting these negative thoughts and emotions rather than sweeping them under the rug, can help us manage our emotions and improve our mental health. Learning to regulate our feelings can make us more resilient and happier.

Researchers have found that people who have good emotion regulation enjoy better psychological and physical health; emotion regulation reinforces our mental strength; practicing self-compassion through emotion regulation aids self-reflection; and emotion regulation improves problem-solving and flexibility; resilience, emotion agility and self-acceptance.

Experts like psychologist Richard Davidson say that people who manage their emotions will have a better grip on their thoughts, actions, and overall well-being. Similarly, Daniel Siegel believes that understanding our feelings through self-reflection can help us become more aware of what makes us tick emotionally.

Psychologist George Bonanno, an expert on resilience, points out that even unpleasant emotions and thoughts play a big role in making us mentally strong. Psychologist, and expert on the topic of emotional agility, Susan David agrees, suggesting that challenging emotions can help us become better problem-solvers. Difficult emotions encourage us to think flexibly and see things from different perspectives.

The benefits of treating yourself with kindness and acceptance in the face of unfavorable thoughts and feelings are revealed by Kristin Neff's research on self-compassion, which leads to increased emotional well-being and resilience. People who practice self-compassion develop a stronger feeling of self-acceptance, cornerstones of self-awareness and self-mastery.

In his book *Social: Why Our Brains Are Wired to Connect,* neuroscientist Matt Lieberman demonstrates that the brain possesses what he terms a mental, physical, and emotional "braking system" that is triggered when we verbalize an emotion. Contrarily, while we frequently hide our emotions, doing so can increase their strength, impede recall, or cause others to perceive us as a threat.

Brené Brown, famous for her work on vulnerability, argues that challenging emotions can help us understand ourselves better and deepen our relationships with others. In her book *Rising Strong,* Brown makes the case that challenging emotions can be a springboard for introspection and personal development.

In his book *Learned Optimism: How to Change Your Mind and Your Life,* renowned psychologist Martin Seligman makes the case that challenging thoughts and emotions can be transformative if people learn to rationalize their negative experiences in an optimistic manner by framing them as temporary, specific, and external.

The Power of Acceptance

Accepting your emotions means letting yourself feel them without judgment. This isn't about giving up or being passive but fully experiencing your emotions.

Acceptance entails recognizing and accepting all feelings, even the negative ones like grief, anger, fear, and anxiety, without passing judgment or trying to alter them. People can make a space where they can see and completely experience negative thoughts and feelings by accepting them.

Why Acceptance Matters

Being able to manage your emotions has several benefits for you. According to research it:

1. **Raises emotional intelligence.** When we practice acceptance, we can better understand our emotional experiences. We can better identify the triggers, patterns, and underlying causes of the emotional states when we allow unpleasant feelings to occur without passing judgment.

2. **Reduces emotional overload.** When we try to suppress or avoid unpleasant emotions, they could intensify or worsen. Contrarily, acceptance could lessen emotional reactivity and enable us to observe these feelings without becoming overwhelmed, encouraging a more logical and controlled response.

3. **Boosts mental flexibility.** Cognitive flexibility is facilitated by acceptance, which allows us to alter our thought patterns in response to challenging emotions. It encourages the adoption of a judgment-free mindset and generating alternative strategies for comprehending and managing negative sensations.

4. **Builds emotional resilience.** With the aid of acceptance, resilience in the face of adversity can be built. Acknowledging and embracing unpleasant sensations can improve our ability to handle difficult situations, recover from failures, and build emotional resilience.

5. **Improves problem-solving.** Acceptance helps us shift our attention from our emotional reaction to problem-solving. It helps us to provide objective appraisals of situations and effective answers to core issues.

Obstacles to Managing Negative Thoughts and Feelings Effectively

You could occasionally find it difficult to deal with your unhappy feelings and thoughts since you are unsure of what to do. Do you need to occupy yourself, try to ignore them? It's crucial first to comprehend where unpleasant feelings and thoughts come from:

☐ **Fear of judgment.** Negative thoughts and feelings are frequently connected to vulnerability and perceived weakness, which causes anxieties of social stigma and judgment. The temptation to maintain a perfect exterior might prevent us from freely identifying and addressing our challenges, as Brené Brown has noted.

☐ **Lack of emotional skills**. Many people lack the knowledge or experience to manage their unfavorable emotions and ideas. IQ is frequently given precedence over emotional intelligence in our society. According to psychologist Marc Brackett, this leads to "emotional illiteracy" and can hinder our capacity to manage unpleasant feelings successfully. One tool that might help is Robert Plutchik's Emotion Wheel, which helps people identify and name their emotions and feelings.

The Emotion Wheel

- [ ] **Cognitive biases and rumination.** Martin Seligman draws attention to our tendency towards negative self-talk, magnifying adverse events and minimizing positive experiences. These cognitive biases can reinforce negative thinking patterns and intensify the struggles associated with negative thoughts and emotions.

- [ ] **Unhelpful coping mechanisms and avoidance.** Individuals may resort to maladaptive coping strategies, like avoidance or suppression, to temporarily relieve negative thoughts and emotions. Psychologists like Guy Win argue that while these strategies may provide short-term relief, they are detrimental to our long-term emotional well-being.

☐ **Insufficient support and resources:** Societal factors, such as the stigma around mental health and the limited availability of mental health services, can prevent individuals from seeking the help they need.

Understanding Cognitive Distortions and Biases

Our sense of reality, emotions, and behaviors can all be distorted by cognitive distortions and biases. These distortions can result from destructive cognitive habits, poor decision-making, and emotional suffering. Cognitive distortions are covered by psychiatrist David D. Burns in his book *Feeling Good: The New Mood Therapy*. In their research, Daniel Kahneman and Amos Tversky showed how cognitive biases might affect decisions.

Here are a few typical cognitive distortions:

☐ **All-or-nothing thinking:** Seeing everything as either completely black or white. Extreme judgments and rigid thinking may result from this.

☐ **Overgeneralization:** Making assumptions based on scant information or a single occurrence.

☐ **Mental filtering:** Concentrating primarily on drawbacks while ignoring advantages.

☐ **Catastrophizing:** Imagining the worst-case scenarios and exaggerating the negative effects of occurrences.

Here are a few typical biases:

☐ **The availability heuristic:** This strategy relies on recent instances or readily available data for making judgments or conclusions.

- ☐ **Anchoring bias.** There is a tendency to base judgments or decisions on the first piece of information encountered.

- ☐ **Overconfidence bias:** Exaggerating our prowess or the precision of our conclusions.

- ☐ **Confirmation bias:** The tendency to favor information that supports our preexisting opinions while ignoring evidence to the contrary.

Positive People are Better at Handling Negative Emotions

Happier people can more easily focus on the positive and successfully deal with the negative. Happier people may be better at appreciating positive feelings and moments to help them cope with stressful situations. They appear skilled at appreciating happy memories and feelings, which helps them deal with difficulties in life more effectively. What does this entail for our perspective on life, though? Does it imply that we should ignore flaws or develop the capacity to emphasize the positive while tolerating the negative? Not so.

Research by William Cunningham and Tabitha Kirkland discovered that happier people had more brain activation in the amygdala in reaction to pleasant photographs when compared to less happy people. But contrary to what the "rose-colored glasses" perspective on pleasure would suggest, they did not exhibit a diminished response to unpleasant imagery. The researchers contend that "happier people are not necessarily naive or blind to negativity, but instead may respond adaptively to the world, recognizing both good and bad things in life."

This is intriguing because it raises the possibility that a key element of happiness may be the capacity to recognize and successfully deal with negative information. The authors' key finding was that "happy people are joyful yet balanced."

You cannot, however, force yourself to feel happy.

Aalborg University professor and *Stand Firm: Resisting the Self-*

Improvement author Svend Brinkmann Craze warns against falling into the trap of never-ending bliss-seeking. He claimed that it might prevent us from developing emotionally. Additionally, happiness isn't always the best reaction in every circumstance.

Brinkmann claims that it's acceptable and right to not always feel happy.

Brinkmann states, "I think our thoughts and feelings should reflect the world. We should be permitted to have unfavorable sensations and thoughts when something awful occurs since that is how we interpret the world." Brinkmann contends that if we strive to be joyful always, we won't be able to handle adversity when it does occur. "There are times when life is lovely but also devastating times. People pass away throughout our lives, and we lose them. If we had only been taught to be permitted to think positively, these realities might have an even greater impact on us when they did occur," he says.

Of course, there are those people who seem to naturally have happier dispositions, but Brinkmann advises against happiness becoming a need and against employers making their staff members constantly happy and optimistic.

Brinkman thinks that society pushes people to keep their worries and issues to themselves because they must always act like everything is fine. Self-help gurus and books that claim we are all responsible for our happiness and accountable for our unhappiness offend Brinkmann. He contends that without the awful things in life, you'd never be able to appreciate the good. It's acceptable to feel depressed, furious, guilty, and humiliated, he says.

Embrace Your Bad Moods: They Can Be Good for You

Feeling down occasionally isn't always bad—it might even be good for you. Throughout history, some of the most impactful works of art, literature and music have been inspired by emotions we generally consider negative. Shakespeare, Beethoven, Chopin, Chekov, and other greats delved deep into the human experience, capturing the full range of emotions, including sadness and despair.

Even the ancient philosophers, who were all about finding the path to a happy life, acknowledged that you can't have the good without the bad. They believed knowing how to manage your feelings and show restraint is the key to a happy life. So, it turns out that feeling bad sometimes might be beneficial.

Recent scientific studies support this timeless wisdom. Research suggests that mild bouts of sadness or irritability can serve as an "emotional alarm system," helping us focus and pay closer attention to details. According to these studies, we're not all affected by bad moods similarly. Some people find value in their bad moods and leave the other side less negatively impacted. People who find worth and meaning in their bad moods seem to experience less of the negative consequences.

Some unfavorable emotions, like melancholy and nostalgia (a yearning for the past), can be enjoyable and offer helpful insight into motivating and making future goals. Sadness can also heighten moral and artistic awareness, empathy, and compassion. And melancholy has long been a catalyst for creative expression in the arts.

After a good cry, you'll feel better.

Ever heard the saying "You'll feel better after a good cry?" A 2011 study of female college students keeping "crying diaries" found that more than 60% felt better afterward. Specifically, 30% reported a boost in their mood. Crying in the company of just one other person, rather than a group or alone, seemed to be the most effective at improving mood.

Does sadness cloud your judgment?

Not likely. Another study showed that when people are sad, they make more detailed and reasoned arguments compared to those who are happy. A 2008 study took it a step further, suggesting that sadness might even make us less gullible. Participants were shown pictures of a car accident and later asked questions about what they saw, some of which were intentionally misleading. The people who were made to feel sad were less likely to fall for the false information compared to their happier counterparts.

When positive emotion follow, bad moods can be inspiring.

A 2011 study that evaluated software developers twice daily for 55 days indicated that individuals who had changed from a negative to a positive mood were more engaged with their job in the afternoon than those who had been pleased or sad all day. The researchers concluded that it is advantageous to comprehend and accept that unpleasant emotions and bad occurrences, such as crises, disagreements, and errors, are essential and inescapable elements of human action at work. Without unpleasant experiences, people will feel less compelled to act and engage in their jobs.

According to Martyn S. Gabel and Tara McAuley's study, having a low mood can improve certain people's executive functioning, including their capacity to concentrate, manage their time, and prioritize their work. According to their findings, there are certain persons for whom being in a negative mood can help them develop critical thinking abilities.

C. Labelling Emotions

How Labelling Your Emotions Can Help You Regulate Your Stress and Anxiety

We've all felt the weight of the pandemic, economic pressures, and feeling cut off from others. With all this happening, it can be a challenge to pin down how we're feeling. Have you ever stopped to think about your emotions in the moment? Many of us might answer with a simple "okay," "fine," or "so-so." But these responses barely scratch the surface of our complex emotional lives.

Researchers have shown that many of us struggle with identifying our emotions. Studies by Kim L. Gratz and Lizabeth Roemer show that it can be difficult for us to precisely name the whirlwind of feelings as we go through daily life.

Naming one's feelings can be more challenging for some people than for others. Vera Vine's and Amelia Aldao's study revealed that individuals who consistently struggle with naming their emotions also struggle with controlling them.

Matthew D. Lieberman, an associate professor of psychology at UCLA, conducted a study that found that merely naming something angry alters our brain's reaction to it. Lieberman refers to this as "affect labelling," according to his fMRI brain scan studies, the amygdala and other emotional brain regions appear to become less active when emotions are labelled. This tamping down of the emotional brain gives its frontal lobe (reasoning and thinking center) more control over resolving the current issue.

According to Lieberman, it's like how you pump the brake when you see a yellow light while driving, it appears as though you are hitting the brakes on your emotional responses when you put sentiments into words. A person may experience less rage or sadness as a result.

According to Lieberman, the world does not operate in accordance with popular psychology's advice to "just pick yourself up" when you are feeling depressed. Self-deception is challenging; therefore, it usually only works if you are aware that you are trying to pick yourself up. He claims that labelling your emotions doesn't have this issue because it doesn't necessitate that you want to feel better.

Mindfulness and Labelling Your Emotions

The Buddhist tradition of mindfulness meditation is now popular in the West. One concentrates on his or her present feelings, thoughts, and physical sensations, such as breathing, while engaging in mindfulness meditation. Dr. Jon Kabat-Zinn, one of mindfulness's early researchers and proponents, defines mindfulness meditation as "paying attention in a particular way: on purpose, in the present moment, and nonjudgmentally."

Labelling your emotions by saying, for instance, "I'm feeling angry right now", "I'm feeling a lot of stress right now," or "This is joy," or whatever the emotion is, is one way to practice mindfulness meditation pay attention to them, according to David Creswell, a research scientist with the Cousins Centre for Psychoneuroimmunology at the Semel Institute for Neuroscience and Human Behavior at UCLA.

The practice of mindfulness meditation has been linked to improvements in a variety of chronic pain diseases, skin conditions, stress-related illnesses, and other conditions, according to earlier research according to Creswell and his UCLA colleagues. He claims that these findings could help explain mindfulness meditation's beneficial effects on one's health and provide, for the first time, a potential explanation for why mindfulness meditation programs improve one's well-being.

By focusing our attention moment by moment and cultivating an interest in our thoughts, feelings, and sensations, the mindfulness practice of observing and labelling aims to help us stand back and observe our mental activity. We step back and watch from a distance, refusing to take credit for the ideas running through our heads. Instead of getting caught up in thoughts or daydreams about the past or the future as we arise, we are attentive to what is happening right now. Instead of reacting, we observe what is happening in our minds, noting how thoughts are expressed, how powerful emotions are felt, and where in our body they are perceived.

When we pay attention to our thoughts, we can notice certain mental activity, such as a particular thought, emotion, or physical sensation, without passing judgment and by simply saying, "I see you," or "Isn't it interesting that this is coming up!" Then, we can return to the present moment by entering our bodies and concentrating on something, like the sensation of breathing or the earth beneath our feet. We can also make ourselves more conscious of the thought, feeling, or sensation by giving it a name.

Labelling is possible casually throughout the day and during a meditation practice. Labelling can be used to settle the mind before beginning a meditation and throughout daily tasks.

Labelling allows us to examine our habitual thought patterns, stand back, and get some perspective. In this approach, we can break the cycle of rumination. It is simple and a great workout for beginning and seasoned practitioners.

During meditation, we select a focus point, such as awareness of the breath or the sound of our footsteps, as in mindful walking. When our minds stray, we compassionately acknowledge the "mental activity," recognize it, and then redirect our attention back to being present with our selected focus point. We merely note that the mind has travelled and that this was the content of the idea without criticizing or analyzing it.

If we are by ourselves, we can use a general "action-verb" label like "thinking" or a more specific label like "planning" or "criticizing," or if the sound is drawing our attention away, we can say "hearing," and then go back to the topic we had initially chosen to act as an anchor for our attention. To further explain what we are seeing, a general "noun" can be used, such as "sensation" (tingling, aching, warm), "thought" (words, image, recollection), "urge" (want impulse), or "emotion" or "feeling" or "sound". You can gain more acceptance by using phrases like "Yes, I see you there" or "Yes to whatever is here."

Keeping in mind that the main objective is to notice, be aware of, and be present simply, it's crucial to avoid concentrating too much on the label you wish to assign. You can use a broad or specialized label if it's clear and simple. Labels are frequently used in hindsight or after the event. You don't have to name everything; only the items occasionally cross your mind. And it's acceptable to keep labelling the same item if that's what you require.

Additionally, we have the option of naming the feeling, such as "calm," "stress," "anger," "fear," "joy," or "calm." When we take notes and categorize things, we can speak with kindness and patience, enhancing the compassion in our inner dialogue. We can choose to address ourselves in the third person. If you want to examine yourself objectively, you can speak to yourself as a friend in the third person by saying, "Hey, Tom, looks like you're feeling angry today."

This designation as a friend may help us feel recognized and understood. It also distances us from what is happening so that we are less reactive. We don't take it quite as personally. We don't have to accept responsibility for anything because it's not our fault; "you are not at fault." This often makes it simpler to put up with and embrace our difficult emotions.

You might feel a "distance" building after the initial experience when you named your thoughts and feelings. Instead of just responding and either lashing out or shutting down, you may (in a few seconds) engage your brain's frontal lobe, calm your body and mind, and choose your response. You can establish connections with both your past and available opportunities. Instead of digging yourself a bigger hole, you can get out of the episode.

As a result, the first step to managing your emotions is to stop trying to ignore them and intentionally start naming them and expanding your emotion vocabulary.

D. How Emotion Affects Your Decision-Making

Everyone wants to make the right decisions. Now, imagine you're asked what the most critical aspect of making smart decisions at work is. Facts? Analyzing risks? Clear-headed thinking? Little influence from emotions?

If you choose the final option, I want you to reconsider after reading this story:

Antonio Damasio's seminal book *Descartes' Error* describes a patient referred to as "Elliot" who had a brain tumor that wounded the frontal lobe tissue in his brain. The result was he couldn't make decisions. Before the tumor, Elliot had a good job at a business firm, was a role model to his colleagues and younger siblings, and was a dutiful husband. After the tumor removal, Elliot's life fell apart. He lost his job, got involved in a moneymaking scheme with a "shady character" that ended up in bankruptcy, got divorced twice, and was denied disability assistance. Damasio discovered that Elliot's decision-making was impaired because he could only use logic to make decisions and couldn't feel emotions.

Damasio says, "Elliot emerged as a man with a normal intellect, who was unable to decide properly, especially when the decision involved personal or social matters." For example, it took Elliot several minutes to decide which color pen to use to fill out his medical forms. It took him over 30 minutes to make his next appointment with Dr. Damasio. And it took him several hours to decide where to have lunch that day.

Damasio referred to Elliott as an "uninvolved spectator" in his own life. "Despite being a major character, there was never any hint of his suffering." Damasio remarked, "I never saw a sign of dissatisfaction, annoyance, or frustration throughout the several hours I spent conversing with him."

Damasio wrote in the prologue to the 2005 edition of his book, *Descartes Error*, "Today this idea [that emotion aids the reasoning process] does not cause any raised eyebrows. However, even though this idea may not be unique to neuroscientists today, the public is astonished by it. We are trained to view emotions as irrational urges that could lead to negative outcomes. When we describe someone as 'emotional,' we typically mean that they lack the ability to make wise decisions. Additionally, popular culture's most logical and intellectual characters are those with the best control over their emotions or who seem to have none."

Even though neuroscience has accumulated considerable evidence over the past 25 years to demonstrate the unbreakable link between reason, emotion, and decision-making, most popular culture still doesn't grasp it.

So, remember that this is impossible the next time someone tells you, "I make my decisions solely based on logic and no emotion (like Star Trek's Spock)."

The "experts" in management still recommend that we make judgments without taking our emotions into account and that employees keep their emotions to themselves while they are at work. Particularly for women, emotionality at work is a strain, and many still feel the need to compensate by suppressing their thoughts and emotions.

Most traditional defences of the superiority of reason over emotion rest on two fundamental premises: first, that we have the option of choosing whether to feel and second, that emotional "suppression" works. Blocking thoughts or feelings outright is a common "regulation" approach, even if there are numerous methods to try to bury or avoid emotions (such as mild to serious addictions of many kinds).

In his research, Daniel Wegner found that suppressing feelings and thoughts can have negative effects. Wegner had spoken of the "rebound" effect. Expressed, these strategies typically fail and intensify the suppressed thoughts and feelings.

So remember this: it is impossible to make decisions without the involvement of your emotions.

How Our Brain Uses Emotions to Decide

Jennifer S. Lerner, Ye Li, Piercarlo Valdesolo, and Karim S. Kassam published a study in the *Annual Review of Psychology* which proposes: "A revolution in the science of emotion has emerged in recent decades, with the potential to create a paradigm shift in decision theories. The research reveals that emotions constitute potent, pervasive, predictable, sometimes harmful, and sometimes beneficial decision-making drivers."

Recent research has revealed several positive elements of emotions in decision-making:

☐ A totally emotional decision is very fast in comparison to a rational decision. This is reactive (and largely subconscious) and can be useful when faced with immediate danger or in decisions of minimal significance.

☐ Some studies suggest our emotions automatically drive our respect for the life of another human being.

☐ Emotions may provide a way for coding and compacting experience, enabling fast response selection. This may explain why expert's "gut" level decisions have high accuracy rates.

☐ Emotions are possible signals from the subconscious that provide information about what we really choose.

☐ Decisions that start with logic may need emotions to enable the final selection, particularly when confronted with near-equal options.

☐ Individuals care about the emotional features of decision options.

☐ Emotions often drive us in directions conflicting with self-interest.

Emotional Decision-Making Can Also Come with Some Negative Consequences:

☐ We make quick decisions without knowing why and then create rational reasons to justify a poor emotional decision.

☐ The intensity of emotions can override rational decision-making in cases where it is clearly needed.

☐ Immediate and unrelated emotions can create mistakes by distorting and creating bias in judgments. In some cases, this can lead to unexpected and reckless action.

☐ Projected emotions can lead to errors because people are subject to systemic inaccuracy about how they will feel in the future.

The continual argument between reason and intuition among pundits is another manifestation of the age-old conflict between reason and emotion. According to science and philosophy author Sam McNerney, the mind is likened to a charioteer who drives two horses, one of which is noble and descended from good stock while the other is irrational and insane, as in Plato's *Phaedrus*. It is the duty of the charioteer to conduct the horses along the way of knowledge and truth. But both horses are necessary.

Our emotional brains are tremendously empirical, and researchers point out that our "emotions are rooted in the predictions of highly flexible brain cells that are constantly adjusting their connections to reflect reality. Every time you make a mistake or come into a new situation; your brain cells are continually changing. Emotions are incredibly clever and constantly changing; they are not just animal instincts that need to be controlled."

Why Finding Balance is the Key

It wastes precious mental resources to debate whether emotion or reason should be used when making judgments. Overthinking frequently overtaxes our brain's pre-frontal cortex, which is responsible for reason. "The Magical Number Seven, Plus or Minus Two: Some Limits on Our Capacity for Processing Information" theory is one of psychology's most highly cited papers by cognitive psychologist George A. Miller. It is often interpreted to argue that the number of objects an average human can hold in short-term memory is 7 ± 2. This has occasionally been referred to as *Miller's Law*. When there is too much information to consider, the brain makes the incorrect decision since its resources are taxed.

We can do things to approach decision-making with more objectivity. The optimal time to do this is right before a challenging decision must be made as a practice to improve the balance between our thoughts, feelings, and actions throughout our daily lives.

Here are Some Strategies for Achieving Balance:

☐ **Monitor your thoughts.** This requires that you keep thinking about your mental process. This involves increasing your awareness of your cognitive process. Make a note of what you are thinking. When you talk to yourself, what language do you use? Is it kind or unkind? Is there a change? If so, when? What decisions do you typically make? Do you frequently overthink, generalize, or even jump to the answer of a problem too quickly? To use this technique, you must be conscious of your thoughts and how you think in different contexts.

☐ **Understand your beliefs and values.** Our values serve as the foundation for all our decisions and actions. They serve as our "rules." Since making decisions typically requires changing our set of rules, we avoid making them. That usually makes us push ourselves past our comfort zones, which is undeniably the realm of our emotions. The first step in spotting thoughts that can impair your decision-making is to understand how you feel about rationalism versus emotionalism.

☐ **Recognize your emotions.** If you don't want to be ruled by your emotions, you must let them be seen and allow them some breathing room. You are wasting precious energy and draining your brain's batteries by attempting to rationalize something that is a bodily experience rather than a logical one when you ignore, downplay, or suppress your emotions. Neuroscientist Antonio Damasio claims that no specific brain area is responsible for decision-making. He claims that the processing of emotions is also controlled by the lower levels of the brain's reasoning framework. Because the lower levels of reasoning and decision-making maintain close, reciprocal relationships with practically every physical organ, the body is actively participating in the series of events that result in the highest levels of reasoning and decision-making.

☐ **Limit your information.** Depending on the scope and significance of the choice, this will change. Numerous studies have shown how having too much information can make it difficult to make decisions. Ensure the information you consider incorporates your intuition regarding the optimal course of action. Studies have shown that your emotional brain can sense the proper path long before your reasoning mind takes control. Since your feeling brain actively listens through your body, the information you occasionally receive could be indirect and somatic.

E. A 5-Step Process Using Emotion Regulation and Rational Thought to Respond Rather Than React

Step 1: Recognize your body's signs. Your body will often respond before your mind. Recognize these signals. Remember your emotions are closely linked to your body.

Step 2: Pause and breathe. We need to provide space—or a gap— between the trigger and the action we take. How do we create space? Take a few deep breaths, count to 10, or wait a few minutes or even hours before acting or speaking. Or take many slow, deep breaths before taking any action.

Step 3: Label the emotion you are feeling. Saying something like, "Oh, there comes anger up in me." Knowing the trigger was someone not treating you respectfully, might be one example. Labelling also helps separate your thoughts and feelings from who you are and reinforces your rational mind.

Step 4: Accept the emotion. This means choosing not to deny or avoid your feelings and acknowledging them without judging them. Instead of wishing things were different or telling oneself you "should" feel differently, this involves accepting the present moment and the feelings you are experiencing.

Step 5: Choose your response. You can now consciously and intentionally decide on the best course of action after creating some space, identifying it, and accepting what "is."

Summary and Follow-up

Self-mastery requires increased self-awareness. An essential component of self-awareness is awareness of our inner thoughts and emotions. One of the most important elements of self-awareness is the capacity to manage your emotions. You can find some strategies and suggestions for managing emotions in Appendix C, which can aid you in your search.

3

Emotional Intelligence

"Some of the greatest moments in human history were fueled by emotional intelligence."

– Adam Grant

Questions to Consider

1. How would you know if you had emotional intelligence skills and attributes?

2. How does emotional intelligence help you in your personal life and career?

3. What is the link between emotional intelligence, self-mastery, and self-awareness?

4. How could you increase your emotional intelligence abilities?

Achieving self-mastery and developing emotional intelligence (EI or EQ) are crucial steps on the path to enlightenment and personal development. Self-mastery is the ability to better understand and interact with your external world and manage and govern your inner state and behavior. The ability to identify, comprehend, and control your own emotions, as well as the emotions of others, is referred to as emotional intelligence.

Emotional intelligence requires awareness of your emotional state, including triggers, patterns, and tendencies. EI may help someone manage and oversee others. Furthermore, it can help kids cope and survive whatever difficulties they may face.

Research

According to Daniel Goleman, a renowned psychologist and researcher and the author of the book *Emotional Intelligence: Why It Can Matter More Than IQ*, a person's emotional and social competence is determined by a variety of essential aspects or components.

The following elements combine to affect how well someone can comprehend, regulate, and use emotions:

- ☐ **Knowing yourself.** Finding and understanding your emotions, strengths, values, and goals are necessary for this. Because they have a full understanding of how their emotions influence their ideas and behaviors, self-aware people are better able to control their reactions, reduce impulsivity, and make more informed decisions. They can react intelligently to diverse situations thanks to this expertise.

- ☐ **Controlling your emotions.** The ability to control and govern your moods, inclinations, and actions is known as self-regulation. It requires managing stress, delaying enjoyment, and adapting to changing circumstances. Self-regulation enables people to control their emotions, react logically rather than emotionally and preserve their composure under duress. It also includes qualities like self-control over impulses and emotional endurance. People can enhance their emotional well-being and create healthier connections by learning self-regulation.

- ☐ **Motivation:** Motivation includes the desire and enthusiasm to pursue goals with persistence and zeal. People with emotional intelligence are driven and self-motivated by a distinct sense of purpose. They set challenging but achievable goals, maintain a positive attitude, and exhibit resilience in the face of challenges. Motivated individuals have a growth mindset and actively seek out opportunities to learn and develop themselves. High motivation has several advantages, including greater productivity and a sense of purpose.

☐ **Understanding others:** True understanding of others involves the capacity to experience another person's feelings. It requires considering the other person's perspective, paying close attention to what they say, and acting with genuine concern and compassion. People with empathy are sensitive to the emotional needs of others and can see things from their point of view. People with empathy tend to have closer relationships with others, negotiate conflicts more effectively, and stand by and comprehend others.

☐ **Social skills:** These abilities related to relationships and interpersonal interactions are called social skills. These qualities are effective communication, active listening, teamwork, influence, and conflict resolution. People with high emotional intelligence are skilled at building relationships, networking, and cooperating in groups. They can lead, inspire, and manage others and excel at creating a joyful and tranquil social environment. Strong social skills are necessary for productive interpersonal interactions, collaborative teamwork, and effective leadership.

The concept of emotional intelligence was invented by psychologists John Mayer and Peter Salovey. Their research laid the foundation for emotional intelligence measurement and understanding. They established the Yale Centre for Emotional Intelligence, which conducts research and provides resources on emotional intelligence.

Research

Since the 1990s, psychologists have emphasized the importance of EI more frequently and the subject has been researched extensively:

☐ According to Graeme Coetzer's study, EQ may be more important than IQ in determining a person's productivity at work.

☐ Raquel Gilar-Corbi and colleagues found that emotional intelligence training enhanced emotional awareness, stress management, mood regulation, and self-expression.

☐ According to research from 2019 by Chad Stevens and colleagues, students with higher levels of EI are often happier, more social, self-confident, and better at handling stress.

☐ According to a review of the literature by Carolyn MacCann studies have shown that EI can aid students in forming social connections in the classroom, which can have a positive effect on their academic progress.

☐ In the book *Eat, Weight, and Conflict* by Una Foye and colleagues, those with lower EQ are less able to control their emotions and are more likely to engage in mood-regulating behaviors that are detrimental to their overall health. For instance, a 2018 study discovered that those with low EI may use alcohol and smoking more frequently as coping techniques and may be more susceptible to eating disorders and self-harming behaviors.

What Indicates Someone Is Emotionally Intelligent?

Anthanasios Drigas and Chara Papoutsi's study identified several essential indicators and instances of emotional intelligence:

☐ The capacity to recognize emotions in others.

☐ An understanding of your strengths and weaknesses.

☐ Self-assurance and acceptance of yourself.

☐ The capacity to forgive errors.

☐ The capacity to welcome and accept change.

☐ A keen interest in other people and their cultures.

☐ Compassion and empathy for other people.

- ☐ Being considerate of other people's perspectives.

- ☐ Assuming responsibility and accountability for behaviors.

- ☐ The capacity to control your emotions amid trying circumstances.

How to Assess Emotional Intelligence

Levels of emotional intelligence can now be measured using a variety of tests. These tests often fall into one of two categories: ability tests or self-report tests.

Here are two measures that may be used in an emotional intelligence exam given by a mental health professional:

- ☐ Mayer-Salovey-Caruso The Emotional Intelligence Test (MSCEIT) examines the four branches of Mayer and Salovey's EI model based on aptitude. Test participants complete exercises to gauge how well they can recognize, interpret, and control their emotions.

- ☐ The Emotional and Social Competence Inventory (ESCI) asks others who know the person to rate that person's skills in several distinct emotional competencies. It is based on an older instrument called the Self-Assessment Questionnaire. The test aims to assess the social and emotional skills that set good leaders apart from others.

Signs of Low Emotional Intelligence

There are several traits, actions, and characteristics that suggest someone has low emotional intelligence. According to scientific investigations, here are some of the signs. They:

- ☐ Always need to be right.

- ☐ Are not considerate of others' feelings.

- ☐ Act without thinking.

☐ Blame others for their problems.

☐ Don't handle stress well.

☐ Get easily upset.

☐ Struggle in their relationships.

The Benefits of Emotional Intelligence

In Western civilizations, we frequently evaluate the value of things and actions based on their benefits, positive results, or outcomes. According to various studies, these are a few outcomes of emotional intelligence.

1. **Better Communication:** People with emotional intelligence can better understand and express their emotions, leading to more meaningful connections.

2. **Stronger Relationships**: People with high emotional intelligence can communicate effectively with others, empathize with others, and forge stronger connections with them.

3. **Effective Leadership:** Leaders with strong emotional intelligence can motivate and uplift their subordinates, get things done, and overcome challenges.

4. **Better Decision-Making:** Effective decision-making involves taking into consideration both cognitive and emotional factors of emotional intelligence.

5. **Better Stress Management:** Emotionally intelligent individuals are more equipped to manage stress and adapt to changing conditions, which enhances overall well-being.

Emotional Intelligence at Work

It's only in recent years that emotional intelligence has been examined in the workplace context—both for employees and leaders. And the findings are significant but still underappreciated.

Researchers such as Nola Extremera and colleagues have found that workers with higher emotional intelligence:

- ☐ Have better people skills.

- ☐ Manage conflicts better.

- ☐ Perform better at their job.

- ☐ Are more satisfied with their job.

Employees who score higher on EQ tests also frequently score higher on assessments of their potential for leadership and stress management, according to a study by Gordon Beenen and colleagues.

In a Career Builder survey, nearly 75% of hiring managers responded that they preferred an employee's EQ over their IQ.

How much does your performance at work depend on your emotional intelligence? Emotional intelligence was the best predictor of performance, accounting for 58% of success across all job categories when the question was put to the test by Talent Smart along with 33 other essential workplace skills.

Ninety percent of top performers at work also possess emotional intelligence, according to Travis Bradbury, a renowned expert on the subject. Only 20% of underachievers, on the other hand, possess high emotional intelligence. Those with high emotional intelligence typically earn $29,000 more yearly than those with low emotional intelligence. Because there is such a high correlation between emotional intelligence and wages, Bradbury claims that every point of increased emotional intelligence increases annual income by $1,300.

Leadership and Emotional Intelligence

Many companies and recruiters still favor charismatic leaders instead of emotional intelligence. As someone who has consulted for senior executives for over 30 years, I've observed a consistent attraction to such leaders. Yet, good leadership involves understanding and managing emotions and demonstrating emotional intelligence.

Leadership is a social interaction process, and performance results can be significantly impacted by a leader's capacity to shape the behavior of their followers. Leadership is fundamentally an emotional process in which leaders identify followers' emotional states, try to arouse followers' emotions, and then attempt to regulate followers' emotions according to those states. Ronald Humphrey makes the case that leaders may boost morale and group cohesion by fostering shared emotional experiences. Furthermore, according to Humphrey, a leader's capacity to affect the emotional climate can significantly impact workforce performance.

A recent study from Virginia Commonwealth University shows a correlation between high emotional intelligence and excellent job performance; in other words, emotionally intelligent people are more productive employees. EQ expert Daniel Goleman studied a connection between leaders' emotional intelligence and their organization's financial success and found there was a direct correlation. Susan David, Christina Congleton, and Steven Wolf have all explored how emotional intelligence benefits teams and their performance.

Summary and Follow-Up

According to the research, emotional intelligence can significantly contribute to creating and maintaining favorable work environments, employee well-being, productivity, and interpersonal connections.

4

Empathy and Compassion

"Give compassion: Every day the average person fights epic battles never told just to survive."

– Ken Poirot

"The highest form of knowledge is empathy."

– Bill Bullard

Questions to Consider

1. How can empathy and compassion develop greater self-mastery?

2. What is the difference between empathy and compassion?

3. What are the elements or components of empathy and compassion?

4. What are the benefits and outcomes for having greater empathy and compassion?

5. How would empathy and compassion help you achieve self-mastery?

Empathy (an element of EQ) and compassion play crucial roles in gaining self-mastery. They facilitate the following:

☐ **Understanding self and others.** By identifying and comprehending the emotions, experiences, and viewpoints of others, this, in turn, provides you with insight into your thoughts, feelings, and motives.

☐ **Regulating emotions.** Compassion and empathy aid in identifying and controlling your own emotions as well as the caring and empathic handling of others' emotions.

☐ **Strengthening connections.** Empathy and compassion enable you to forge strong and meaningful connections with others.

☐ **Fostering altruism and purpose.** Compassion and empathy directly relate to having a sense of direction and meaning in life. Altruism and acts of kindness not only help those around us, but they also give our lives meaning and fulfillment.

A. What is Empathy?

Empathy is about stepping into someone else's shoes. It requires us to see from the other person's perspective and respond with feeling and understanding. It goes beyond merely feeling sorry for the other person, which is pity or sympathy. The ability to relate to others effectively requires emotional intelligence, which requires self-awareness as a prerequisite. The American Psychological Association (APA) defines empathy as "understanding a person from his or her frame of reference rather than your own, or vicariously experiencing that person's feelings, perceptions, and thoughts."

Daniel Goleman says that "empathy is a fundamental aspect of emotional intelligence that enables individuals to connect with others and navigate social interactions effectively."

Empathy must not be confused with compassion, which is characterized as "a profound awareness of another's suffering coupled with the desire to relieve it," or sympathy, which is "a relationship or an affinity between people or things in which whatever affects one likewise affects the other." In a piece for *The Economist*, empathy expert Jamil Zaki refers to empathy as "the psychological superglue that connects people and supports cooperation and kindness."

Kinds of Empathy

According to Daniel Goleman, there are three distinct types of empathy. The first is cognitive empathy, the intellectual understanding of another person's thoughts, feelings, and opinions. The ability to understand another person's emotional condition is known as emotional empathy, which is the second. Compassionate empathy, the third sort of empathy, is displayed when we want to help others based on our understanding of their needs and feelings.

How Do You Recognize an Empathetic Person?

Researchers have identified some behaviors that increase empathy. Empathetic people:

- ☐ **Listen actively:** A person with empathy hears what the other person has to say first and speaks only thereafter. Empathic people use active listening to comprehend others, which includes asking themselves questions like, "From what I hear you saying, it seems to be..." and asking, "And then?" as well as nodding and smiling.

- ☐ **Offer vulnerability.** People with empathy frequently share a personal story about a situation or problem like the current one. They become more likeable as a result, and the situation softens.

- ☐ **Don't make assumptions.** Assumptions limit their capacity to empathize. To be truly empathic, they must let go of preconceived notions that are not supported by knowledge or personal experience.

- ☐ **Use their imagination.** There is no way you could have experienced every situation others discuss with you. So, utilize your imagination to understand better how the other person is feeling. It's a great idea to try to understand a character whose situation is completely different from your own by reading fiction literature.

☐ **Pay close attention to other people.** When with empathic people, you frequently feel like the only person in the room. They interact with people by showing them the special gift of their respect and undivided attention, which is unusual in today's too-distracted culture.

☐ **Are aware of nonverbal cues.** What is being said cannot be properly expressed by words alone. If you notice someone tensing up, stepping back, or abruptly avoiding eye contact, you can use empathy to reach out. Ask them to explain what is going on nicely rather than dismissing how they are feeling. People are free to openly express their emotions since they are confident they won't be judged or criticized for doing so. Being emotionally liberated can make it easier to solve problems effectively.

☐ **Get accustomed to silence.** We often try to be helpful by interjecting, giving advice, or finishing others' sentences. Empathic people are aware of the strength of quiet. They don't interrupt or talk over other people. They wait before they speak.

☐ **Ask questions rather than offer suggestions.** Instead of stating their own opinion, empathic people prefer to make enquiries to understand more about another person's perspective.

☐ **Are aware of the pain of others.** They demonstrate their awareness of other people's needs and capacity to recognize changes in other people's behavior.

☐ **Recognize their own pain.** Distress tolerance is the ability to endure or contain uncomfortable emotions. Some people may simply walk away when faced with another person's pain, refusing to offer support or take the necessary measures.

☐ **Retain appropriate eye contact.** Making eye contact with others improves communication success and makes them feel seen. and being conscious of cultural variations in eye contact.

☐ **Identify their own and other people's emotions.** We can better grasp an empathic person's behavior or the meaning behind their words and sentiments by understanding their feelings and giving them names.

☐ **Are conscious of their voice tone.** Since tone of voice accounts for more than 38% of nonverbal emotional content in communication, developing empathy is crucial. They will feel heard if you talk in a soothing voice and match the volume and tone of the person you speak to. You should temper your tone when someone expresses wrath rather than adopt it.

☐ **Appropriately respond rather than react.** How we relate to the person we're speaking to is very important. We frequently synchronize emotionally with others, whether intentionally or unconsciously. It is essential to be able to manage their emotional reaction to prevent merging with the other person or acting in an unhelpful manner.

Is Empathy Inborn, or Can It Be Learned?

Both! **From the moment they are born, babies show signs of empathy.** Ever notice how one crying baby can set off a roomful of other infants? It's not just about the noise. Research shows babies react differently to another baby's genuine cry than a fake one.

The way children are raised makes a difference. One study by Ruth Feldman and colleagues showed that babies with more physical contact with their mothers developed stronger empathy as they grew. And according to the findings of their meta-analysis of 18 empathy training trials, empathy may be taught.

We can cultivate empathy throughout our lives and use it as a powerful tool for social change, according to Roman Krznaric, founding faculty member of The School of Life in London, empathy advisor to organizations like Oxfam and the United Nations, and author of *The Wonderbox: Curious Histories of How to Live and How to Find Fulfilling Work.*

Since ancient times, there has been an underlying assumption that people are born inherently bad. It's a concept that shapes news reports, television programs, motion pictures, and the laws that govern our daily lives. The origins of this idea can be found in various works of Western philosophy, including those of Machiavelli, Thomas Hobbes, Sigmund Freud, and, some would claim, the Bible and Christianity. We've been taught that people are inherently egocentric and primarily motivated by their own interests.

Rutger Bregman's *Humankind: A Hopeful History* is one of the best works that argues that empathy is an innate human trait. In his analysis of the past 200,000 years of human history, Bregman argues that humans are inherently kind and empathic, not competitive but rather cooperative, and more prone to trust than distrust one another, explaining how this exists across many cultures. Homo sapiens' evolutionary history provides a solid evolutionary foundation for this tendency, Bregman says.

A team of developmental psychologists under the direction of Julia Krevans point out that most of the past research has focused on how much sharing occurs among toddlers of objects that are already theirs. Their new study shows toddlers frequently display extraordinary justice and kindness.

In a different study, 112 three-year-olds were observed exchanging resources and awards in psychological science in teams of two males and two girls. The sharing in over 80% of these cooperative scenarios was "passive," meaning that one child got the two fair rewards and left the other for his or her partner. The other child would occasionally be instructed to take their fair share of the pie if they didn't do so right away. Other times, one child would deliberately take two rewards and hand the other two to the other two. Physical altercations and disagreements were hardly ever present.

None of these altruistic gestures would have been possible without the existence of empathy.

"The present excitement surrounding empathy is a result of a significant shift in the science of how we understand human nature," according to Krznaric, "Evidence suggests we are not just homo sapiens but also *homo empathicus*—wired for empathy, social collaboration, and mutual aid—pushing the traditional thinking that believes humans are essentially self-interested creatures to the side."

In the last ten years, neuroscientists have learned that our brains have an "empathy circuit" that, if damaged, can restrict our ability to understand how others feel. Evolutionary biologists like Frans de Waal claimed that we are social animals who have evolved and thrived as a species to care for one another.

Researchers A. Senju and colleagues claim that before 18 months, we are already predisposed to feeling empathy.

Jamil Zaki's book *The War for Kindness* states, "Our collaborative flair stems from empathy: the capacity to share, understand, and care about what others feel. People who can empathize easily report better levels of contentment, lower levels of stress, and simpler social interactions. Everyone involved benefits from these positive effects: patients of empathic doctors are happier with the care they receive, spouses of empathic people are happier in their marriages, children of empathic parents are better able to control their emotions, and employees of empathic managers suffer from stress-related illnesses less frequently. Empathy maintains the social fabric of our society by encouraging altruism, tolerance for those who are different from us in appearance or ideology, and commitment to environmental sustainability."

Why Business Needs An Empathy Revolution

We've all heard about cutthroat workplaces where bullying is rampant. Politics today is infused with mean and hurtful people. Racism, crime, and abuse still is prevalent.

Even in financially successful firms, we increasingly hear reports of toxic workplaces and toxic leaders where rudeness, abuse, and bullying are the norm. Never in history has the need for empathy and compassion for others been stronger, both within organizations and in society at large.

Simon Baron-Cohen, a professor of developmental psychopathology at Cambridge University, is one of the foremost experts on the psychology of empathy. His book, *The Science of Evil* explores what he has learned about the link between empathy and cruelty over more than two decades of research.

Baron-Cohen argues that those who exhibit a greater lack of empathy and who lack the need to make apologies after harming someone else—what he refers to as "Zero-Negative"—have abnormal brain patterns, which explains why they are capable of harm and, in certain cases, commit the most terrible crimes.

Studies utilizing fMRI technology support Baron-Cohen's hypothesis. With the aid of this technology, scientists have been able to go inside the heads of psychopaths, who are most inclined to commit crimes of a sadistic type and have found severe anomalies in their brain activity. For instance, when shown images of people suffering, psychopaths' brains undergo reduced activity in regions important to the empathy circuit, according to fMRI scans.

Another study found that watching movies about individuals getting wounded caused reward-related brain activity in adolescents with high levels of aggression. This demonstrates that individuals with antisocial personality disorder may have a lack of empathy as well as take pleasure in witnessing the misery of others.

"I See You"

"Sawubona," a Zulu greeting that is translated as "I See You," means "We See You." An adaptation of the idea appeared in the motion picture *Avatar*. It's a way of understanding that people's perceptions, which are molded by both their own experiences and the myths and ideas that have been ingrained in them through their family and culture, play a role in how they interpret the world around them.

Why Businesses Should Care More About Empathy

Most business schools and employee training programs focus on the "how" to do your job—the cognitive processes and job skills. They rarely if ever focus on emotional intelligence, empathy, compassion, and kindness. And leaders are chosen based on either their knowledge and expertise or because they are charismatic.

According to current studies, business executives and students seem to have lower levels of empathy. Sarah Brown's research hints that business students seem more self-centered than students in other fields. They're also more likely to cheat—and by a big margin. This isn't just about classroom ethics. Brown suggests these attitudes might carry into the professional world, which could explain some damaging corporate behaviors we've seen.

Karoline Strauss at ESSEC Business School examined the same topic and concluded: "Research has shown that students majoring in economics are less concerned with the benefits of others. The more economics courses students take, the more positively they view self-interest and the better they feel about their self-interested behavior. It seems learning about economics fosters more positive attitudes towards selfishness."

Roger Karnes claims that "empathy and social skills are undertrained and underdeveloped by organizations." His research discusses the negative spiral effect that starts with ineffective leadership, leads to a general lack of social skills and empathy in businesses, manifests as mistreatment of employees, and ends with rising employee discontentment and all its effects.

Wendy Mill Chalmers draws the intriguing conclusion that, given the challenges of the current fast-paced organizational climate, there ought to be a positive correlation between hard criteria and soft abilities. In 'faster' workplaces, she says, inspirational leadership that demonstrates emotional intelligence, sensitivity, and understanding of the development requirements of its staff members is more important than "hard" technical skills.

According to Chalmers, if modern leaders want to go beyond simply adapting to modern norms, they must engage in "21st-century enlightenment." She examines the ideology of possessive individualism, which has come to be associated with consumer capitalism and democracy. She finds that it has promoted selfishness, greed, and unethical behavior while devaluing empathy.

If you think your workplace successfully exhibits empathy, think again. Less than 50% of employees believed that their firms showed empathy, according to recent *Businessolver* research.

For 46 years, Development Dimensions International (DDI), a training industry pioneer, has studied leadership. They believe that the key to effective leadership is having several "fruitful conversations" with people inside and outside your organization. To find the conversational skills that have the biggest impact on performance, they assessed more than 15,000 executives from more than 300 companies across 20 industries and 18 countries to provide evidence for this claim.

According to DDI study, there is a critical need for empathic leaders. In their thorough examination, only four out of ten frontline leaders exhibited high or adept empathy.

In an interview with *Forbes,* Richard S. Wellins, senior vice president of DDI and one of the study's authors, said, "We feel empathy is significantly declining. Even more concerning is that a University of Michigan survey of college students over eight years found a 34 to 48 percent loss in empathic skills. Future leaders will come from these students! We think that one reason for this reduction is that leaders now have a lot on their plates from their organizations, which makes them less likely to connect face-to-face."

Studies on Leader Empathy

Many modern leadership theories contend that empathy is crucial to effective leadership. Transformational leaders need empathy to demonstrate to their followers that they are concerned about their needs and success. Genuine leaders must also possess empathy to be considerate of others. Many experts agree that emotional intelligence, including empathy, is essential for a successful leader.

The following findings about the importance of empathy in leaders come from other studies:

- ☐ Leaders who truly connect and understand their teams often witness more enthusiastic and productive behaviors.

- ☐ Teams get more creative when their bosses showcase qualities like humility and empathy.

- ☐ Empathy boosts leadership. Different leadership styles, from charismatic to servant leadership, highlight their importance. Dynamic interpersonal skills produced by empathy inspire workers and increase leaders' effectiveness.

- ☐ Empathy isn't just a feeling. It has deep roots in our brains. For instance, watching someone get hurt might make us wince because our brains have evolved to feel that pain.

- ☐ Self-awareness is the foundation for empathy. Empathy goes beyond only expressing emotion; it also requires thinking and feeling.

Empathy and Self-Awareness

Researchers go into great depth about how empathy and mindfulness are related, including the following:

- ☐ Mindfulness helps us be in the moment and accept experiences different from our own, which can help grow our empathy.

- ☐ Experts like Christopher K. Germer and Ronald D. Siegel believe that mindfulness helps us feel more connected to everything around us, breaking down barriers we often put up.

- ☐ Early research has shown that mindfulness-based therapies have the potential to promote empathy in close relationships.

Boosting Our Empathy

You can become more empathic, even if you may not have experienced that early in life, or focused on it as an adult.

Roman Krznaric's has spent a decade studying empathy. He believes making empathy a regular habit can enhance everyone's life. Here's what he recommends to grow our empathic muscles:

1. **Get curious about others**. Engage with strangers. Chatting with someone new can broaden our understanding of different lifestyles. It's like reigniting the curious child within us.

2. **Believe in growth.** Researcher Erika Weisz from Harvard says the first step to being more empathetic is believing we can be.

3. **Experience another's life.** Try stepping into someone else's shoes. For example, author George Orwell once lived among the poor in East London, which transformed his views and relationships.

4. **Listen deeply.** Being a good listener is more than just hearing words. It's about truly understanding the emotions and needs of the speaker. That's empathetic listening.

5. **Ask questions.** Instead of thinking you know what someone is saying, empathy pushes you to have an open mind and ask questions to ensure you understand them. Asking questions is the key to comprehending someone else's perspective.

6. **Pay attention to body language**. Words are just part of the story. Notice the voice tone, facial expressions, and body movements to understand others' emotions. Even better, mirror them.

7. **Share relatable stories.** Sharing a time when you underwent a similar experience can show the other person that you listened to what they had to say and understand their feelings. They could feel less alone in their situation as a result. However, act

with caution here. Never attempt to "one-up" someone by bringing up a time when you, too, had a quarrel with a close friend or got rejected from a job that you wanted.

8. **Read fiction (not non-fiction).** Dive into a good novel. It's like a practice session for empathy as you understand a character's emotions and actions. What better way to develop empathy than to read a novel or short story and put yourself in the other person's shoes?

9. **Connect with different cultures.** Engaging with diverse groups helps us see the world through different lenses. Even simple interactions can broaden our empathetic perspective. According to some commentators, Americans' unwillingness to travel outside of their home nation is a sign of their intolerance and prejudice toward people of different racial and cultural backgrounds. In a study conducted by market analysts OnePoll under contract with the travel accessory manufacturer Victorinox, 2,000 Americans found 11% of poll participants have never been outside of their home state, 54% have only visited 10 or fewer states, 13% have never travelled in an airplane, and 40% have never left the United States.

10. **Improve emotional recognition.** Understand the fine lines between emotions and feelings, for example, the difference between frustration and disappointment. Learn the vocabulary of emotions.

11. **Take an empathy assessment.** The University of California, Berkeley's Greater Good Science Centre provides a free online empathy test that quickly assesses your level of empathy.

B. Compassion

What is compassion? How does it differ from empathy or doing good deeds? While empathy refers to our ability to feel and understand the emotions of others, acts of kindness, such as donating to charities, might not always stem from genuine compassion or empathy. Compassion is a deep feeling we get when we see someone suffering and have an authentic desire to help.

Compassion is essentially about wanting to alleviate someone's struggles or pain. It's a core human value that benefits individuals and our larger communities. Spiritual teachings worldwide prize compassion, while modern science emphasizes its importance for our well-being and survival as a species.

Many believe that the concept of "survival of the fittest" comes from Charles Darwin. However, Darwin spoke more about sympathy as the strongest instinct in humans, essential to our survival and the cornerstone of our ethical systems.

More recently, psychologist and primatologist Frans de Waal has compiled a large body of evidence showing moral behavior and deeds performed by non-human primates. He contends that these behaviors date back to at least the last common ancestor of birds and mammals and that this is where the roots of compassion can be found.

If we define love as the desire for the joy of another, then compassion and love are two sides of the same coin. When we are emotionally attached to someone, we experience love and compassion because we want them to be happy and pain-free.

The Science of Compassion: Origins, Measures, and Interventions conference looked at the development and pace of scientific research into compassion. The four days of discussion (which were organized by Stanford's Centre for Compassion and Altruism Research and Education) yielded the following key insights:

1. **Safety first.** Compassion thrives when we feel safe, both physically and psychologically. Only when our more ingrained "self-preservation" and "vigilance-to-threat" systems (such as fear, distress, anxiety, and hostility) are not occupying center stage can the biological mechanisms that drive our nurturing and caregiving activate.

2. **Mindfulness is essential for compassion.** Being present and truly engaged now, especially regarding others' suffering, nurtures compassion. Actively practicing compassion can also make our brains more attuned to positivity. Harvard academics Daniel Gilbert and Matthew Killingsworth have shown that this pervasive non-mindful behavior diminishes happiness.

3. **Taking compassionate action activates the brain's pleasure center.** Additionally, taking compassionate action—such as giving away a portion of your profits to charity—activates pleasure circuits, often known as "the warm glow." For instance, the "carryover effect" describes how showing compassion to others causes the brain to be biased toward taking in more good information from the outside environment.

Can You Become a More Compassionate Person?

Can you become more compassionate? Yes! While we naturally feel more compassion for those close to us, with effort and intention, this circle of compassion can expand.

Our interconnectedness is often overlooked, but realizing how many people contribute to our lives can spur gratitude and compassion. To make this realization transformative, it requires active practice and learning.

Researchers at the Waisman Center's Centre for Investigating Healthy Minds at the University of Wisconsin-Madison found that adults can learn to be more compassionate. The study is the first to investigate whether promoting altruistic behavior in adults might alter the brain circuits that underlie compassion.

What are the Benefits of Compassion?

Research has shown that compassion has great advantages for our well-being, including our physical and mental health; it may have assured our survival. Compassion provides a multitude of benefits both for the recipients of compassion as well as the givers.

Connecting with others meaningfully improves our mental and physical health and has been shown to hasten the recovery from disease, according to research by Ed Diener, and Martin Seligman. Additionally, research by Stephanie Brown at Stony Brook University and Sara Konrath at the University of Michigan has described the many benefits of compassion.

Emma Seppälä Ph.D provides a comprehensive summary of the research on compassion in *Psychology Today*, where she says: " Though economists have long argued the contrary, a growing body of evidence suggests that, at our core, both animals and human beings have what Dacher Keltner at the University of California, Berkeley, calls a "compassionate instinct." In other words, compassion is a natural and automatic response that has ensured our survival.

Giving sweets to others makes people happier than receiving them yourself, according to research by Lara Aknin and colleagues at the University of British Columbia, as shown in their work with toddlers. Even more interestingly, regardless of whether a nation is wealthy or impoverished, giving makes us happier than receiving.

Living a compassionate life may also reduce stress, which is another way it can lengthen life. Michael Poulin of the University at Buffalo led a recent study that found compassion is so enjoyable that it is one of the ways that it could prevent stress. However, it appears that motivation is a key factor in determining whether leading a compassionate life improves health. University of Michigan researcher Sara Konrath found that those who volunteered lived longer than those who did not, but only if their motivations for doing so were altruistic rather than selfish.

The ability to see beyond ourselves is another way that compassion may improve our well-being. However, when you do something for someone else, that self-focus condition switches to a state of other attention. Research suggests that sadness and anxiety are linked to a state of self-focus, a concern with "me, myself, and I." while a close friend or relative calls you for immediate assistance with a crisis while you are already feeling down, you may remember that your mood improves as your focus switches to assisting them. You might have been motivated to help instead of feeling down, and before you realized it, you might even have felt better and reflected on a perspective on your own life.

Finally, establishing a sense of connectedness to others is another way that compassion may improve our well-being. According to one eye-opening study, social isolation negatively impacts health more than obesity, smoking, and high blood pressure. On the other hand, the study found, that people with strong social connections had a 50% higher probability of living longer. According to studies by Steven Cole, social connection affects genes that code for immune function and inflammation, which improves our immune system, speeds up the healing process after illness, and may even increase our lifespan.

Self-Compassion

Imagine a friend who's going through a difficult time. You'd likely offer words of comfort, maybe a hug, and listen to their woes, wouldn't you? Self-compassion is doing the same thing but for yourself.

When you encounter adversity, suffer failure, or become aware of your shortcomings, self-compassion includes treating yourself with the same kindness. Instead of pushing your suffering aside with a "stiff upper lip" attitude, you pause and reflect, "This is difficult right now," "How can I comfort and care for myself in this moment?"

When faced with personal failings, self-compassion means showing compassion and sympathy rather than severely critiquing and criticizing oneself for your flaws.

The most important aspect of cultivating self-compassion is acknowledging and accepting your humanity. Not everything will always go as planned. In life, you will be let down, lose money, make mistakes, come up against your limitations, and fail to achieve your goals. This is a universal reality about human nature that all people share. As you learn to open your heart to this reality rather than constantly fighting it, you will be able to feel compassion for yourself and every other person engaging in the experience of life to a greater extent.

Self-Compassion's Three Elements:

☐ **Being empathetic and kind to yourself.** Self-compassion involves being gentle and empathetic toward ourselves when we struggle, falter, or feel inadequate instead of ignoring our suffering or hurting ourselves with self-criticism.

☐ **We are all human.** Frustration at not receiving what we desire frequently goes hand in hand with an illogical but pervasive sensation of isolation—as if "I" were the only one having problems or making mistakes. But pain affects everyone. Realizing that "external" factors like family history, culture, genetic make-up, environment, as well as other people's behaviors and expectations, have an impact on us is another requirement.

☐ **Distancing your identity and self-image from outside factors.** If we had total control over our behavior, how many people would consciously choose to have issues with eating disorders, crippling social anxiety, poor anger management, and other issues? Numerous (genetic and/or environmental) elements that we have little control over contribute to many aspects of who we are and the circumstances of our existence. Therefore, because we don't equate those outside situations with our inner selves, mistakes and difficulties in life don't have to be taken so personally but can instead be embraced with non-judgmental compassion and understanding.

☐ **Being mindful.** Self-compassion also requires a balanced approach to our unpleasant feelings to prevent exaggerating or suppressing them. When you are mindful, you can acknowledge your thoughts and feelings without trying to deny or suppress them. To prevent falling prey to our own reactive behaviors, mindfulness encourages us to avoid becoming "over-identified" with our thoughts and feelings.

What Self-Compassion is Not

Self-pity causes people to focus on their own problems and ignore other people's struggles. They disrespect their relationships with others and think they are the only ones going through difficult times. Self-pity has a propensity to exaggerate one's own suffering and enhance egocentric feelings of loneliness. On the other hand, self-compassion allows you to observe your own and others' shared experiences without these feelings of exclusion and alienation.

The difference between self-compassion and self-indulgence is also extremely clear: "Yes, what I'm going through right now is incredibly painful, but many other people are suffering far more. Maybe it's not worth getting all worked up over."

Many people assert that they are reluctant to engage in self-compassion because they worry that if they did, they would let themselves get away with anything. But instead of self-compassion, this is self-indulgence: "I'll just watch TV and eat a quart of ice cream all day since I'm stressed out today." In many situations, giving yourself simple pleasure can be harmful to your health (e.g., using drugs, bingeing, or being lazy), but providing yourself with long-lasting health and pleasure frequently involves some discomfort (e.g., quitting smoking, dieting, or exercising).

People are frequently quite hard on themselves when they observe something they want to change because they think self-flagellation will make them act. This tactic, however, usually backfires if you can't face uncomfortable truths about yourself because you're so afraid of developing self-hatred. As a result, mistakes could be overlooked in an unconscious attempt to win sympathy. As a powerful driver for growth and change, on the other hand, the caring that is at the core of compassion also provides the security needed to evaluate yourself honestly without concern for self-criticism.

Leadership and Workplace Compassion

Can the operating system of an organization be compassion?

Men have dominated business organizations for at least the last 200 years. Male-oriented values and behavioral traits, such as competitive hostility, dispassionate problem-solving, rationalism, and logic, have been the organizational drivers in line with this. On the other hand, historically speaking, so-called "soft skills," such as teamwork, cooperation, and loving affection, have been considered more typical of women and as "weaknesses."

Organizational behavior literature has seen radical changes over the past three decades emphasizing the importance of emotions for employee attitudes, interpersonal connections, and emotional intelligence. However, this research has mainly disregarded the core feelings of compassionate love, such as feelings of attachment, compassion, empathy, caring, and kindness toward others.

P.J. Frost asserts that "as organizational researchers, we tend to see organizations and their members with little other than a dispassionate eye and training that inclines us toward abstractions that do not include consideration of the dignity and humanity of those in our view." He adds, "We lose touch with and miss the humanity and 'aliveness" of organizational life when our emotions and sympathies are not fully engaged".

Organizational structures, HR practices, and training and development methods that incorporate compassion for employees are naturally excluded from or discounted in organizations where cold, rational behavior predominates. It is uncommon to find leadership development programs or staff handbooks that strongly emphasize compassion, kindness, and tolerance. Additionally, when a CEO acts in a transactional and detached manner, it spreads. As a result, when numerous businesses utilize it, a standard for the company is created. The financial benefits of logical, heartless corporate procedures are undeniable, but at what cost to relationships, employee morale, and happiness?

In a piece for the Greater Good Science Centre at the University of California, Berkeley, Emma Seppälä, Science Director of Stanford University's Centre for Compassion and Altruism Research and Education, Co-Director of the Yale College Emotional Intelligence Project at the Yale Centre for Emotional Intelligence, and author of *The Happiness Track*, discusses the rising incidence of workplace stress among employees. She argues that new research shows that companies that promote an "ethic of compassion rather than a culture of stress" may have a better workplace and an improved bottom line.

According to Emma Seppälä's essay in the *Harvard Business Review* "compassion and curiosity increase employee loyalty and trust." According to a study she cites, an employee's loyalty is more influenced by their coworkers and their positive emotions than by their pay.

New York University researcher Jonathan Haidt found that employees are more loyal to their bosses when they have a higher level of regard for them and are touched by their generosity and compassion, a condition he named "elevation." Therefore, by treating your employee with greater compassion, they will be more loyal to you, and everyone else who witnesses it will feel the same way.

Claudio Fernandez-Araoz argues in *Harvard Business Review* that organizations should promote a "culture of compassionate coaching," which goes beyond merely pointing out staff members' shortcomings. He also asserts that encouraging a "culture of unconditional love" improves collaboration.

Tim Sanders makes the argument in his book *Love Is a Killer App: How to Win Clients and Win Friends* that "those of us who use love as a point of differentiation in business will separate ourselves from our competitors just as world-class distance runners separate themselves."

Sigel G. Barsade and Olivia A. O'Neill from the University of Pennsylvania found that employee contentment, absenteeism, and emotional exhaustion positively correlate with teamwork and compassionate love. Most leadership and organizational culture literature, according to Barsade and O'Neill, has largely disregarded emotions since it is thought that love "stops at the office door and that work relationships are not deep enough to be called love." They also assert that "no organizational theory incorporates behavioral norms, values, and fundamental presumptions about the nature of emotions and the effects they have on workers."

How Leadership in the Modern Capitalist Era Lacks Compassion

According to Hershey H. Friedman, a leadership crisis in the world today is affecting business, government, and education. The lack of moral character displayed by the leaders worries everyone, especially young people. Corporate executives seem to be more concerned about finding ways to raise their own compensation than they are with making sure that workers receive fair compensation. Despite all the discussion about CSR and business ethics, many corporate leaders don't care about ensuring employees are treated fairly.

Summary and Follow-Up

In the present, which is marked by such turmoil and harm to both people and the environment, empathy and compassion serve as the glue that holds the self-mastery crucible together as they are important elements of emotional intelligence.

5

Prosocial Behavior

"We have so far to go to realize our human potential for compassion, altruism and love."

– Jane Goodall

Questions to Consider

1. What is meant by prosocial behavior?

2. How does it contribute to self-mastery?

3. What are the characteristics of prosocial behavior?

4. What are the benefits and outcomes of prosocial behavior?

Prosocial behavior is any action taken to assist others. These deeds can be little, such as holding a door open for someone, or more major, such as volunteering for a good cause. It includes being kind, empathic, cooperative, and generous and altruistic. Prosocial behavior can take many forms, such as sharing resources, offering emotional support, volunteering, or participating in charitable activities.

Intentional prosocial behavior training can help people learn to prioritize the needs of others, manage their emotions, and develop empathy and compassion—all of which contribute to greater self-awareness. The relationship between self-mastery and prosocial behavior has been supported by research from various fields, including psychology, neuroscience, and philosophy.

According to Abraham Maslow, a psychologist best known for his "hierarchy of needs," the highest level of self-mastery, self-actualization, frequently involves transcendence or helping others achieve self-actualization. This is how prosocial behavior can result in personal growth.

Richard Ryan and Edward Deci, psychologists and academics have known for their contributions to the self-determination theory, assert that prosocial behavior is connected to three core psychological needs: relatedness, competence, and autonomy. They argue that self-mastery is essential in promoting prosocial behavior because it helps people act according to their values and make choices that benefit others.

According to psychologist Angela Duckworth, self-mastery is a key element in supporting prosocial behavior over the long run. The research Duckworth conducted on grit and self-control is well known. According to her, those who have better self-control are more likely to stick with their prosocial goals in the face of difficulties or setbacks.

In their study, Grant J. Rich and Kristin D. Neff discuss the significance of self-mastery in fostering prosocial behavior. They contend that self-mastery is not possible or at least it is incomplete if individuals operate primarily out of self-interest.

According to Dacher Keltner, a psychologist at the University of California, Berkeley, leading a prosocial lifestyle can lead to acts of kindness, compassion, and gratitude that improve self-mastery.

Prosocial behavior, according to Sonja Lyubomirsky, a pioneer in the field of positive psychology, benefits both the giver and the recipient. According to her, helping others enhances our sense of competence and self-worth while also bringing about happiness and a sense of purpose.

The Elements of Prosocial Behavior

- ☐ Compassion and empathy.

- ☐ Altruism.

- ☐ Cooperation.

- ☐ Helping.

☐ Generosity.

☐ Unexpected reciprocity.

☐ Moral reasoning.

Here are the benefits and outcomes of prosocial behaviors according to several research studies, which include an overall sense of well-being and mental health, reduced conflict, and building stronger communities.

Some Typical Prosocial Behaviors

☐ Volunteering for worthwhile causes or charities.

☐ Sharing your material goods with those in need.

☐ Donating to worthwhile causes or charities.

☐ Doing something to improve our environment (city or country, e.g., planting trees).

☐ Helping the elderly or disabled.

☐ Helping friends, neighbors, or co-workers with tasks.

☐ Being an organ donor.

☐ Giving blood to the Red Cross.

☐ Living a less materialistic lifestyle.

☐ Becoming adept at conflict resolution.

☐ Committing to peaceful, non-aggressive and non-violent behavior.

☐ Acting in an ethical manner.

Benefits and Outcomes

☐ Mood-boosting effects: Research has also shown that people who engage in prosocial behaviors are more likely to experience better moods.

☐ Social support benefits: Social support can be crucial for overcoming difficult times.

☐ Stress-reducing effects: Research has also found that engaging in prosocial behaviors helps mitigate the negative emotional effects of stress.

☐ The well-being of others and a community are advanced.

☐ Prosocial beliefs and philosophy can become an integral part of organizational culture.

☐ Improved self-esteem, life satisfaction, and general mental health.

Social Media's Role

Platforms like Facebook and Twitter can be great tool for prosocial behavior.

This communication route not only enables platforms to inform, assist, and support all regions of the world suffering from natural disasters, it also provides a rapid means of demonstrating recognition globally. Examples might be giving money to a worthwhile cause or participating in climate change activist protests.

Making people aware of issues such as climate change and drawing more attention to it can inspire others and change their perspectives on it for the better. One instance was when people used Facebook and Twitter to donate money and show support for one another during the relief efforts following the 2011 Thoku earthquake and tsunami off the coast of Japan. Anyone may directly contribute to the Japanese relief effort on Facebook's The Red Cross fan page and through internet coupon sites like Groupon and LivingSocial.

The "feel good-do good" phenomena, in which being in a good mood boosts prosocial behavior, enables us to perceive the "good" in others and prolongs our good mood, is something that many individuals encounter. For instance, studies on the relationship between mood and behavior at work suggest that helping coworkers is one of the most beneficial work-related behaviors associated with a positive mood at work.

Numerous research studies have shown how volunteering and other prosocial behaviors can improve self-esteem, life satisfaction, and general mental health. A negative mood might also affect prosocial behavior. In contrast to other negative mood states like dread, guilt can initiate prosocial behavior, according to one study.

Bryant P.H. Hui and colleagues reviewed 126 prior studies with close to 200,000 individuals in a meta-analysis. They discovered that informal prosocial behavior, such as volunteering for a cause at a set time, had less of a beneficial effect on well-being than more spontaneous prosocial behavior, such as helping an elderly neighbor carry groceries.

Another study found that cultivating positive emotions like thankfulness may help promote prosocial behavior. According to a study by Monica Bartlett and David DeSteno, gratitude enhances efforts to assist a benefactor even when those efforts are costly (i.e., hedonically negative). This increase, however, is fundamentally distinct from efforts undertaken due to having a generally upbeat emotional state. They also show how gratitude could lead to aiding strangers rather than only people with close social relationships.

Why Kindness Is Needed in the World

In our competitive world, winning at all costs is valued highly. The popularity of critical pundits, egotistical heroes, and public insults, especially on social media, proves this. Aggression, cynicism, and criticism are frequently regarded as traits of the "superior" individual. Being kind is frequently viewed as a flaw.

Unbalanced Media Coverage

Even though there were positive stories about the kind and supportive responses of people and communities and commentary about the need to take proactive action to bring safety and security to communities, most of the news coverage of tragic events focuses on the negative aspects — pictures of the scene of the carnage, police, weapons, and experts providing endless detail about the events and people — and ignores the positive aspects.

Prosocial behaviors "are buffers for the negative effects of stress, likely through strengthening the positive interpersonal connection. In previous laboratory-based studies, simply watching kindness media uplifts (elevates) viewers, increases altruism, and promotes connection to others," according to a study by David A. Fryburg and colleagues.

How Watching Harmful Behavior Can Affect Us

Douglas A. Gentile co-authored a study that found watching aggression including bullying in movies and TV, may prime the brain for aggression. According to Gentile, "What this study demonstrates is that relational aggression can actually alter your thinking, which is important because, of course, your thinking can alter your behavior." One of relationship violence's most publicly publicized effects has been the growth of cyberbullying, which Gentile calls a classic example of the practice.

In a world of growing complexity, competition, intolerance, and impatience, there are calls for a more respectful form of leadership in business and society — leadership that promotes a sense of inclusion, connection, and belonging.

What Does it Mean to Be Kind?

The dictionary defines kindness as the "ability to demonstrate generosity and consideration towards others." In other words, true kindness is not selective; it is shown to others irrespective of who they are, based on the understanding that we all have something important in common: being human. Being kind means showing consideration, compassion, and understanding toward everyone, not just those we know and love.

Human kindness is a core value in many religions, including Christianity, Confucianism, Taoism, and Hinduism. Although we may not be able to identify specific or individual acts of kindness that occurred thousands of years ago, we have reason to believe that they have always been present in society, whether in the form of religious and spiritual beliefs, or as social norms and expectations.

To promote kindness, Houston Kraft, the author of *Deep Kindness: A Revolutionary Guide for the Way We Think, Talk, and Act in Kindness*, has created Character Strong, a curriculum and training organization that has given him a platform to work with schools worldwide.

Popular science books like Franz De Waal's *The Age of Empathy: Nature's Lessons for a Kinder Society* have confirmed what Darwin observed: humans have an enormous capacity for prosocial behavior.

Many websites are dedicated to spreading kindness, organizations embracing it, and educational initiatives to cultivate our better nature. Scientific reviews, such as Sonja Lyubomirsky and Kristin Layous' paper in *Current Directions in Psychological Science,* claim that people can increase their happiness by practicing kindness.

Some countries have embraced kindness. The values statement of the Scottish Government is "We are a society which treats all our people with kindness, dignity, and compassion respects the rule of law and acts openly and transparently." Kindness is one of the key performance indicators in the new framework, which outlines the purpose of the government and identifies outcomes that all public institutions must achieve.

According to research compiled in Penelope Campling's book *Intelligent Kindness: Reforming the Culture of Healthcare,* individual acts of kindness release endorphins and oxytocin and form new neural connections. For example, she discovered that increased activity in the posterior superior temporal cortex has been reported in altruistic individuals (when compared with less altruistic individuals).

A study by Melanie Rudd, Jennifer Aaker, and Michael I. Norton found that, "Small, concrete goals designed to improve the well-being of others are more likely to lead to happiness for the giver than actions with large, abstract goals-despite people's intuitions to the contrary."

Kindness can positively alter your brain by increasing levels of dopamine and serotonin, which give you pleasure, satisfaction, and a sense of well-being. When the recipient of your kindness responds with kindness, it can increase self-esteem, empathy, and compassion, improve your mood, and even help you live longer. Kindness can increase your sense of connectivity with others, lessen loneliness, and enhance relationships.

"We found that any kind act appeared to have the same benefit, even small gestures like opening a door for someone or saying 'thanks' to the bus driver," write Lynn Alden and Jennifer Trew in their study.

Being Kind Starts Early

While most earlier studies on children's kindness focused on how much toddlers shared things they already owned, a current study examines how often they shared brand-new items that no one else previously possessed. According to developmental psychologists led by Julia Ulber, infants regularly exhibit outstanding generosity and justice in such circumstances.

According to Michael Tomasello, co-director of the Leipzig, Germany-based Max Planck Institute for Evolutionary Anthropology, young human toddlers are naturally cooperative and helpful.

According to a study from the Institute for Learning & Brain Sciences at the University of Washington, or I-LABS, kindness may develop as early as infancy. Researchers found that children will provide delectable food to a stranger in need even if hungry in a study of over 100 19-month-olds.

Kindness at Work

When we think of business, kindness isn't the first thing that springs to mind; instead, we frequently envision images from early 20th-century industrial America, a time of hard work and demanding employers. Work required correctness and managerial control, employee monitoring and corporate authoritarianism, vigilance and icy objectivity and interpersonal distance.

According to conventional thinking, every company needs a calculating CEO, focused solely on the company's financial goals, and possibly competitive to the point of being overly aggressive and confrontational. In this new era of competition, we presume that managers who are unable or unwilling to cut costs ruthlessly, constantly drive staff, and be unyieldingly tough are too compromised to survive in a hard, competitive climate.

A study by Katherine Nelson and colleagues demonstrated that workplace kindness increased people's feelings of autonomy and competence. Additional research has found that kindness fosters greater workplace well-being, boosting employees' energy levels, optimistic outlooks, and problem-solving abilities. According to one study, people treated well at work reciprocate the favor by being 78% more kind to their coworkers than a control group.

Kindness in Leadership

Good leaders know the importance of being kind. Treating employees with respect, listening to their concerns, and leading with compassion are all crucial. It creates a positive environment where everyone feels valued. When leaders are kind. It creates a culture of giving and support throughout the organization. During the pandemic, many leaders discovered that kindness was their secret weapon to keep teams motivated.

"Organizations benefit from actively fostering kindness," stated Ovul Sezer, Kelly Nault, and Nadav Klein in a *Harvard Business* Review paper.

People receive acts of kindness, study reveals — and not just to the same person, but frequently to someone completely different, leading to a culture of generosity in an organization. The spillover effects can snowball quickly in workplaces where acts of kindness become the norm.

According to Boris Groysberg, a professor at Harvard Business School and journalist Susan Seligson,"The pandemic has challenged managers like never before, but one powerful leadership strategy is being overlooked: Be kind." The authors consulted 200 leaders from big and small businesses in the public and private sectors worldwide. Some of these leaders were alumni of the Oxford Advanced Management and Leadership Program at the Said Business School. In contrast, others were drawn from the authors' wide networks, which included EFMD and the European Women's Management Development Network (EWMD) members.

These leaders from around the world emphasized that kindness in leadership has a universal appeal and is defined by a variety of kindness-based behaviors, including adopting a humane approach, fairness and equity, accommodating personal issues, treating others with respect, caring and being responsive, communicating with a personal touch, transparently sharing information, explaining logically, and listening intently.

Richard Davidson of the University of Wisconsin likened acts of kindness to weight training: "People can build up their kindness 'muscle'" and respond to others' suffering with care and a desire to help," he said, "Great leaders affirm that being consistently pleasant, encouraging, and genuinely concerned about employees' mental health during tough times is not a sign of weakness or ceding control."

In fact, leading with kindness is the most effective leadership style to spur innovation and competitive advantage in the market, according to the ground-breaking Humankindex Survey of U.S. workers. Signature Consultants, a renowned supplier of IT and professional staffing and solutions, carried out the survey. It discovered a definite link between the exercise of kind leadership and a business' capacity to foster and encourage innovation.

In its first annual release, the Humankindex for all U.S. corporations with a Kindness Quotient of 31.5/100. Employers in the United States believe that when there are qualities of compassion present in the culture and leadership, such as:

- ☐ 78% more likely if the company regards compassion as one of its core values.

- ☐ 5X more likely if employees believe their work has some relationship to the company's goals and direction.

- ☐ 28% more probable if the company employs "leading with kindness."

- ☐ In general, employees are 5X more likely to view companies with higher Kindness Quotient scores as innovative.

How to Encourage Leaders to Lead With More Kindness

The pandemic's widespread effects necessitate a more compassionate approach to management and leadership. What can CEOs and managers do to bring compassion and empathy to their leadership? Here are some quick, practical tips for being kind every day:

"When someone shares that they're struggling, you won't always know what to say or do," write Kelly Greenwood and Natasha Krol in the *Harvard Business Review.* The most crucial thing is to create space for your team members to communicate their true feelings, and to show compassion. They might not want to disclose much detail, which is also acceptable. Here are some examples they provide:

- ☐ **"Are you alright?** Be prepared to provide support, watch for signs of distress including social withdrawal and poor performance, and know when to refer a worker to a professional for help.

- ☐ **"What can we do to assist?** Being kind and compassionate can be as simple as acknowledging an employee's difficulties during the epidemic or as complex as actively pushing mental health options or creating a virtual support group or sounding board.

☐ **"How are things doing for you these days?"** Some companies are gaining a deeper understanding of their workforces' unique challenges by polling home workers." They've found that working remotely as a single person has a very different set of pressures than working as a working parent with young children.

☐ **"I'm here for you."** Consistently let your team know you are available for them when they need to discuss difficulties or a sympathetic, nonjudgmental ear. Consider being available outside typical working hours; these are not usual.

☐ **"I know you're doing the best you can."** People are reporting they are working harder than they did before COVID in many first-person accounts and on social media. This makes perfect sense; as layoffs and furloughs skyrocket, employees fear losing their jobs. In times of crisis, bosses must adjust their expectations.

Altruism

Altruism is the act of promoting the welfare of others without seeking any personal gain or benefit, even at a cost to yourself. Altruistic actions are motivated by empathy, compassion, kindness, and a sincere desire to help.

Altruism typically emerges from the ability to understand and share the thoughts of others and the desire to alleviate suffering. Altruism is driven by a true care for others rather than acting for self-gain.

Altruism involves taking action to help others through acts of kindness, volunteering, or making sacrifices; it is not just an idea or attitude. Altruistic actions are performed without any expectation of compensation or acknowledgment.

Altruism has been shown to increase your sense of purpose, happiness, and general well-being, according to research. By fostering a sense of belonging, building trust, and creating deep connections with people, altruism can deepen social ties and relationships. Research shows that being altruistic might improve physical health and reduce stress.

Summary and Follow-Up

The world cries out for greater compassion, kindness, selflessness, and altruism. I challenge you to become one of those who have made this personal commitment. We can all give one single gift to one single human individual to make this life more tolerable and brighten the future of humankind.

6

Resilience

"It's your reaction to adversity, not adversity itself that determines how your life's story will develop."

– Dieter F. Uchtdorf

Questions to Consider

1. How do you deal with adversity and setbacks?

2. What negative events do you find most difficult to bounce back from?

3. How do you develop greater resilience?

4. What are the benefits and outcomes of resilience?

5. What are your self-limiting beliefs?

6. What is the downside of perfectionism?

7. How do you deal with failure?

A. Resilience

Have you ever wondered how some people manage to bounce back from difficult or traumatic circumstances, while others struggle? That ability to recover and move forward is called resilience.

Resilience is crucial because it allows people to maintain their wellness and flourish despite challenges.

Resilience and self-mastery go hand in hand. Possessing qualities that promote resilience, such as emotional intelligence, tenacity, and problem-solving skills, are also necessary for achieving self-mastery. Self-mastery can increase resilience. When one can regulate their impulses, emotions, and behaviors, one can better handle challenges and recover from setbacks.

A resilient person can gather their resources, solicit help when needed, and devise solutions to their issues. People with psychological resilience can adjust to many challenges in life, such as those related to:

- ☐ The passing of a close friend or relative.
- ☐ A divorce.
- ☐ Financial worries.
- ☐ Poor health.
- ☐ Loss of a job.
- ☐ Medical emergencies.
- ☐ Natural disasters.

Instead of giving in to hopelessness or using unhealthy coping methods to escape issues, resilient people face life's obstacles head-on.

Those who are resilient experience distress, grief, and worry just as others do. Instead, they employ healthy coping methods to deal with these difficulties and typically emerge from the situation stronger than before.

Characteristics of Resilience

- ☐ **A survivor mentality:** Those who are resilient identify as survivors. They are aware that if difficult circumstances do emerge, they can overcome them.

- ☐ **Effective emotional regulation:** Resilient people often exhibit this trait, but it doesn't mean they don't also go through intense emotions like anger, grief, or terror. When under stress, resilient people can keep their emotions under control. It suggests that they are aware that those feelings are transient and may be managed until they pass. Resilient people possess a strong feeling of self-control and the conviction that their actions can change the way things turn out.

☐ **Accepting flaws and imperfection**. Being aware of and accepting the fact that perfectionism makes resilience more challenging.

☐ **Self-compassion:** Another sign of resilience is exhibiting self-acceptance and compassion. Resilient people are compassionate to themselves, even in trying circumstances.

☐ **Dealing effectively with failure:** The capacity to respond constructively to failure.

☐ **Effective decision-making:** Understanding and practicing the elements of good decision-making, particularly the influence of emotions.

☐ **Growth mindset:** Adapting from failures to advance. being observant.

☐ **Adaptability and flexibility**: Steering clear of inflexible, set-in-stone attitudes and actions undermining resilience.

Some Research on Resilience

Psychologists call the ability to walk through bad experiences 'resilience'. "It generally means adapting well in the face of chronic or acute adversity," says neuroscientist Dr Golnaz Tabibnia, who studies the neurological basis of resilience at the University of California, Irvine.

Dr. Eric Meyer and his team from the Department of Veterans Affairs in Waco, Texas have shed light on an interesting discovery within the American military veteran community. Through studying veterans of the Iraq and Afghanistan wars, they noted that individuals who showed fewer signs of post-traumatic stress disorder (PTSD) — which could be seen as a testament to their resilience — often exhibited a characteristic called "psychological flexibility." This means they tended to disagree with statements like "I am afraid of my feelings" and "emotions cause problems in my life."

In simpler terms, psychological flexibility is like emotional adaptability. Dr. Selda Koydemir, a psychologist and counselor not involved in Meyer's study, explains that being psychologically flexible involves changing our perspectives and actions during tough times without feeling totally overwhelmed. It doesn't mean avoiding hard emotions but embracing them as a natural part of our experiences. Dr. Koydemir emphasizes that staying engaged with these difficult experiences, while approaching life's challenges with an accepting and adaptable mindset, can make us more resilient and direct us towards a more meaningful existence.

A crucial part of psychological flexibility is also knowing what's truly important to us, like our values and major life goals. This means that, despite facing hardships, we keep our focus on actions that drive us towards achieving these objectives. In essence, if enduring discomfort assists them in chasing their meaningful goals, psychologically flexible people are usually ready to welcome such uneasy states.

But how does psychological flexibility interact with our experiences beyond war zones? It seems to also be a pivotal element during widespread crises, such as the COVID-19 pandemic. Dr. Nima Golijani-Moghaddam and Dr. David Dawson from the University of Lincoln aimed to understand emotional coping during such hard times by surveying over 500 UK citizens in May 2020, during a period of stringent nationwide lockdowns.

In the context of overwhelming and continual shifts, fear, and uncertainty brought about by the pandemic, Golijani-Moghaddam and Dawson explored how psychological flexibility might serve as a buffer, or a form of resilience, under these harsh conditions. Although their survey found an expected spike in anxiety levels (27% meeting anxiety disorder criteria, as opposed to the typical 6% in normal circumstances), those individuals with higher psychological flexibility seemed to navigate through with lesser anxiety or depression. They even reported feeling an overall higher sense of well-being.

In both scenarios - military veterans and citizens amid a pandemic - psychological flexibility stands out as a key attribute in managing emotional well-being during trying periods. Understanding and potentially cultivating this ability to "roll with the punches" emotionally could be a tool for all of us in managing future adversities.

In her book, *The 5 Practices of Highly Resilient People: Why Some Florish When Others Fold*, Neuro-psychologist Taryn Marie Stejskal argues that "challenge fundamentally and forever changes us." Encountering adversity or trauma permanently changes our brain structures through plasticity. There is nothing to return to; resilience is an active process, not passive. Stejskal argues "While time does lessen the sting of wounds, losses and grief, residence is not about merely waiting passively for time to pass. To effectively face the challenge and harness resilience, you get to show up and be present as an engaged participant," and resilience is about connecting deeply to our internal selves. Stejskal says "Hustle culture has done a number on us, making many of us believe that the recipe for success is a 24.7 all-on work life. . . . Resilience is still being used as a reason for people to ignore their burnout, stress level or exhaustion in favor of 'pushing through.' This constant expectation of productivity is to tony detrimental to our health, happiness, and relationships, it is toxic and damaging."

Numerous other research studies have emphasized the importance of resilience in life. For instance, in a research study by K.M. Connor and J.R. Davidson, they found resilience is linked to lower levels of anxiety and depression, improved physical health, and higher levels of life satisfaction.

A Word of Caution About the Belief That "What Doesn't Kill You Makes You Stronger"

Resilience doesn't mean you are necessarily stronger because of your experience with adversity or trauma. In fact, the reverse may be true according to recent research.

According to recent research, the opposite is true: traumatic experiences in the past make people more vulnerable to future traumas and raise their risk of mental health disorders.

For instance, according to several US government publications, PTSD affects 15 to 30% of US veterans who have served in the military. They did not become more resilient as a result of their painful experiences.

According to a recent study, some of the most reliable indicators of whether a patient hospitalized for COVID-19 would continue to have symptoms of extended COVID a year later included the death of a loved one, food or financial insecurity, or the onset of a new handicap.

Studies of the long-term effects on mental health for POWs in war zones indicate ongoing and sometimes life-long damaging effects resulting in a variety of mental health problems.

A study from Brown University is calling into question the validity of that statement. The researchers reported that past traumatic events usually make people more sensitive and vulnerable to future problems, not more resilient.

More than 100 scientific studies have examined this question. The highest-quality studies have surveyed people before adversity and then studied them again afterward. Those studies have found that adversity doesn't regularly lead to genuine posttraumatic growth. Deepening relationships is the only type of growth that seems to arise consistently from adversity. During times of struggle, our relationships with loved ones often become more intimate, meaningful, and rewarding.

So the research evidence shows that people do *not* usually experience positive personality change as a result of adversity. Instead, their personality usually stays roughly the same. Or, in some cases, they might even experience declines in certain areas, such as their self-esteem or their spirituality.

So the takeaway from the research is that while we can build resilience through certain beliefs and behaviors that doesn't necessarily mean that trauma and adversity are a recipe for resilience and strength.

How Can We Develop Greater Resilience?

According to many studies, you can use several tactics to become more resilient. Here are a few examples:

☐ **Adopt a positive view:** Positive psychology expert Martin Seligman claims that re-framing issues and adopting a positive outlook can boost resilience. This includes maintaining a positive outlook and focusing constantly on solutions rather than problems.

☐ **Establish a support system:** Resilience requires a strong social support system.

☐ **Develop your capacity for problem-solving.** This includes the capacity to develop habits, create objectives, make choices, and communicate clearly.

☐ **Practice self-care.** Taking good care of your physical, mental, and emotional needs is essential for resilience. Participating in relaxing activities, including exercise and mindfulness, can help with stress management and resilience.

☐ **Improve your flexibility and adaptability.** Resilience includes the ability to adjust and be flexible in the face of change. Carol Dweck's growth mindset research highlights the importance of accepting problems and seeing them as opportunities for learning and growth.

☐ **Reframe unfavorable concepts.** Resilient people may see positive events realistically, but they do it without blaming others or fixating on unchangeable truths. Adversity shouldn't be viewed as insurmountable; instead, change your perspective and seek constructive adjustments.

☐ **Establish your life's purpose.** Take steps to define, uphold, and strengthen your life's purpose after giving it some thought.

☐ **Help others.** To improve your sense of worth and purpose, practice prosocial and altruistic behavior.

☐ **Take a break for yourself.** The tension you are presently feeling could get greater if anything bad happens in your life. Your emotions may already be erratic due to hormones and physical changes, but the uncertainty that comes with a tragedy or trauma can make these shifts feel even more pronounced.

A new study found that mindfulness boosts resilience. Researchers Badri Bajaj and Neerja Pande discovered that mindful people have higher psychological resilience. The researchers also provide evidence that this very beneficial characteristic is why many of the practice's well-lauded benefits exist. The researchers concluded due to how we perceive and respond to stressors: "Mindful people... can better cope with difficult thoughts and emotions without becoming overwhelmed or shutting down (emotionally)."

Being Adaptable at Work

Resilience has also been researched in connection to failure and setbacks in the workplace. Since psychological resilience is one of the cornerstones of good organizational behavior and since workplaces are becoming more disruptive and demanding, scholars' and practitioners' attention to this topic has greatly increased. Studies have identified several personality traits, personal resources (like self-efficacy, work-life balance, social competencies), personal attitudes (like sense of purpose, job commitment), positive emotions, and work resources (like social support, a supportive organizational context) as potential promoters of workplace resilience.

What Characteristics Define Resilient Leaders?

Margaret Wheatley contends that resilient leaders should pay attention to the people affected by fast change and stress within the firm instead of focusing on the organization's structure. Resilient leadership promotes a focus on the people expected to work with the change rather than depending on a system or structure because people tend to become easily overwhelmed when experiencing change.

Furthermore, resilient leaders look for ways to deal with continuing, unknown future change and the irreversible changes that have already occurred. Resilient leaders focus on identifying solutions for inescapable change and researching potential changes.

Jennifer Garvey Berger contends in her book *Simple Habits for Complex Times: Powerful Practices for Leaders that* good teams recover quickly from setbacks and maintain optimism and composure, and their leaders work to alter people's mindsets. She argues that resilience in a complicated and rapidly changing world requires more than simply recovering from setbacks. Leaders need to evolve and develop each time they make a comeback. According to Berger, a resilient leader must be able to accomplish more than persevere through hardship.

According to a study by Kenneth E. Lane, Thomas McCornack, and Michael D. Richardson: "In today's world, resilient leaders look for ways to manage in an imbalanced world where the focus is on leading for resilience, where the future is unpredictable, where capacity is uncertain, and where learning is social."

A Personal Note About Resilience

My personal life gave me an opportunity (although not voluntarily) to experience and understand resilience at a profound level.

My family (mother, father, sister, and brother) were prisoners of war incarcerated by the Japanese in WWII in Stanley Internment Camp in Hong Kong for almost four years (1941 to 1945). I was born in Stanley Camp in 1945, almost perishing along with my mother. The story of my family's survival and the resilience skills and attitudes that my father and mother taught us through example and conversations have been invaluable to me, something that I have attempted to pass on to my children.

While the trauma and subsequent PTSD that came from that wartime experience, the resilience that my parents demonstrated will live with me until I die.

B. Self-Limiting Beliefs

Your incomplete or faulty assumptions or perceptions about who you are and how the world works are examples of self-limiting beliefs. These assumptions are "self-limiting" since they keep you from fully controlling yourself.

How Do You Form Beliefs?

From a young age, we start to form ideas about the world and our role in it. This is because our brains are designed to recognize patterns and make connections. Most of the time, our earliest beliefs come from our parents or other important adults in our lives, and they're based on our personal experiences. For example, if you find out that hitting someone has negative consequences, you start to believe that it's wrong to be physically aggressive. Similarly, saying "please" and "thank you" gets positive reactions, so you start to think being polite is good.

As we grow up, our beliefs become more complex and influenced by many other factors, like friends, TV shows, books, and movies. But often, we hold onto the core ideas we formed when we were younger because they're deeply ingrained in us.

Many people develop self-limiting beliefs, thinking they're failures or not good enough, often without concrete evidence to support these thoughts. Studies have shown that such beliefs can be misleading and may not be based on rational analysis. People with these negative mindsets often find it difficult to change them.

Psychologist Robert M. Williams explains that beliefs act like filters through which we see the world. Just as camera filters affect a photo's appearance, our beliefs shape our perspective on life. You may see yourself as valuable or worthless, strong or weak depending on your beliefs. These beliefs impact everything from your emotional well-being to work performance and physical health.

Your beliefs can be either conscious or subconscious. Think of your mind like a computer: while you may be aware of some "software programs" running in your brain, much of this software operates in the background, in your subconscious. According to Harvard Professor Emeritus Gerald Zaltman, research shows that about 95% of our thoughts and decisions come from our subconscious level. That means our subconscious beliefs greatly influence how we act and react to life's challenges, even if we aren't fully aware of them.

In his book, *The User Illusion: Cutting Consciousness Down to Size,* Tor Nørretranders reveals that while the conscious mind can process about 40 bits of information per second, the subconscious mind can handle about 40 million pieces of information in the same time frame.

What About False Beliefs?

What exactly qualifies as inaccurate or wrong beliefs? We have erroneous and restricting views about ourselves, others, or objects. They live in our subconscious mind, and since 90% of everything we do originates there, our false ideas tremendously influence practically everything we do. Because they are subconscious, we might not know how they affect our daily lives.

For instance, if you believe you are unlovable, you might damage relationships, stay in them when you shouldn't, or refrain from beginning any. Our behavior is influenced by our beliefs. And our way of life is a result of our group efforts. Therefore, if we change or discard our beliefs, especially those that are false, we may change our behavior and, ultimately, our lives.

Your feeling of self-worth can be damaged by any unfavorable or self-critical beliefs about yourself, which can also keep you from benefiting from rewarding opportunities, connections, or experiences. Self-limiting views are those that hold such thoughts.

What Are the Sources of False/Self-Limiting Beliefs?

The most important programming for the subconscious mind is received during the first six years of life. The child's brain is "downloading massive amounts of information about the world and how it functions during that time (birth to age six)," according to Dr. Bruce Lipton, Ph.D., cellular biologist, and author of the book *The Biology of Belief.*

It is important to understand that perceptions acquired before age six become the fundamental subconscious programs that shape an individual's life. Adult EEG readings from brains show that neural electrical activity is correlated with different states of awareness. The human brain operates on at least five frequency levels, each associated with a different brain state.

The predominance of delta and theta activity expressed by children younger than six indicates that their brains are operating at levels below those of adults. A child's brain activity ramps up and operates primarily in the range of theta between the ages of two and six, which corresponds to the state where children spend a lot of time fusing the real world with the imaginary.

The first six years of a child's life are spent in a hypnotic trance. When, as young children, we "download" limiting or sabotaging beliefs, those perceptions or misperceptions become our truths, and delta and theta brain frequencies define a brain state known as a hypnagogic trance, the same neural state that hypnotherapists use to directly download new behaviors into the subconscious minds of their clients.

Your mind keeps returning to the thought, emotion, or memory of how you behaved in the initial incident, reinforcing the self-limiting attitude whenever you reflect on the past or have a conversation with someone. You were told you weren't competent or good enough to do or be something or someone by a higher authority figure—your parents, siblings, instructors, or teen friends.

Kinds of Limiting Beliefs

Self-limiting statements like "I am uncoordinated," "I'm not pretty," "Men are only out for one thing," "Families are dysfunctional," and "Success is a matter of luck" are all phrases you may recognize by the verb "am," "is," or "are." You should take some time to think about this.

Self-Deception

Since a person may have a totally irrational picture of their own situation and their internal state, self-deception can be a major obstacle to achieving self-mastery.

We all practice self-deception daily, but what possible profit could we possibly receive from misleading ourselves? You probably wouldn't believe it if I told you you've lied to yourself more than anyone else.

Self-deception is advantageous from an evolutionary and psychological standpoint.

As strange as it may sound, self-deception occasionally results in the development of positive traits like resiliency, optimism, and self-assurance.

We can better handle the threat in our immediate environment by convincing ourselves that it is insignificant.

Self-deception may appear advantageous, but it also encourages negative self-talk and self-image, limits your capacity for growth, and keeps us from actively looking for solutions to our problems.

Self-deception is the act of lying to oneself about one's capabilities, skills, and challenges as well as lying to oneself about one's external events and realities. A great experiment by Zoe Chance, an associate professor of marketing at Yale University, demonstrated that many people inadvertently use self-deception to raise their egos.

Self-deception has two elements: the denial of reality and the unawareness of the denial of reality. When someone lies to themselves, they come to believe the lie to be true and accept it as truth. Psychologists claim that self-deception can be seen as a form of defence and self-preservation, either on the outside or as a defence against stress, worry, or other negative emotions.

Self-deception makes it difficult for someone to deal with situations or employ effective change management approaches because it impairs their ability to think clearly and view things realistically.

Self-Deception Red Flags

- ☐ **Denial.** The refusal to accept the reality of the situation or your own position.

- ☐ **Minimization:** Minimizing the gravity of the situation or the false claim.

- ☐ **Rationalization.** The act of trying to give an alternative justification for wrongdoing, deviant behavior, or socially unacceptable behavior.

- ☐ **Projection.** When someone lies to themselves, they convince themselves that the problem is with someone else.

- ☐ **The "Imposter Syndrome."** People deceive themselves about their skills or abilities because they feel unworthy or fraudulent.

- ☐ **Holding others responsible for your errors.** People deceive themselves by upholding a positive reputation and avoiding accountability.

- ☐ **Closed off to constructive criticism.** Self-deceivers are prone to escalating their hostility and defending themselves.

Cognitive Distortions

Cognitive distortions are ideas that cause people to have false perceptions of reality, and according to psychologist Aaron Beck's cognitive model, emotional dysfunction symptoms and lower subjective well-being are rife with cognitive distortions. Cognitive distortions are thought patterns that are exaggerated or unreasonable and contribute to the development and maintenance of psychopathological states, particularly those that are more strongly impacted by psychosocial factors, such as depression and anxiety.

Out of the many that exist, the following are a few of the most typical cognitive distortions that can influence limiting beliefs:

- **Filtering, overgeneralization, catastrophizing, fortune telling, and bad prediction**: You magnify in your mind the negative specifics of a situation while excluding all positive or neutral aspects of it. You draw a general conclusion based on a few instances or pieces of evidence. For example, if something negative occurs once or twice, you assume it will occur more frequently. You assume failure or the worst-case scenario.

- **Polarized thinking:** You see things as either good or bad, in black or white, and there is no room for ambiguity or doubt. An even more extreme variation is believing there is only one option available. One type of polarized thinking is perfectionism, which requires that your decision or behavior be flawless. Another type is extremism in politics or religion, which demands that your action be faultless.

- **Control fallacies:** You believe you can and should control other people or events in the outside world. This impulse to exert control usually results from a need to affirm your value, sense of security, or self-worth. Anger or anxiety frequently accompanies the craving for control.

- **Entitlement.** You act as if someone is keeping score, and you expect all your sacrifice and self-denial to be rewarded. When the reward does not appear, you become resentful. You think you should be subject to different laws governing others. Because your mental or emotional state depends on external circumstances, this is also known as the fairness, reward, and entitlement fallacy.

☐ **"Should" (and "shouldn't"):** There is often judgment, criticism, and guilt. You have unbreakable rules governing how you and others should behave. You get upset when people break the rules and feel bad if you break them yourself.

Among the many methods and strategies for overcoming limiting beliefs include mindfulness, cognitive behavior therapy (CBT), cognitive restructuring, rational emotive behavior therapy, positive affirmations, and the understanding that thoughts are not truths.

C. Perfectionism

Striving for perfection can act as a roadblock to achieving self-mastery. While our society often commends perfectionists for their high standards and tireless commitment, their achievements can come at the cost of prolonged dissatisfaction and unhappiness.

Renowned psychiatrist David Burns writes in *Psychology Today* about the potential pitfalls of perfectionism, noting, "While perfectionists aim high, they often fall short, which can lead to unstable relationships and mental health concerns."

Some positive traits are associated with the perfectionist personality type, so it is best thought of as a multifaceted feature. In its maladaptive form, perfectionism pushes people to strive for impossibly high standards or lofty objectives, which frequently results in burnout.

The weight of self-imposed unrealistic goals invariably ends in disillusionment, and perfectionist can be excessively critical of themselves when they don't meet their own benchmarks. They often peg their self-worth to their achievements and are consumed by the pursuit of these goals.

Psychologist Thomas S. Greenspon distinguishes between "striving for excellence" and perfectionism. He contends that while perfectionists often feel they must be flawless to be valued, this aspiration to perfection is not beneficial. In his view, terms like "healthy perfectionism" is a misnomer. Authors Jeanette Dewyze and Allan Mallinger, in their book, *Too Perfect: When Being in Control Get Out of Control*, describe perfectionists as having obsessive personality traits.

"There's a difference between excellence and perfection," asserts Miriam Adderholdt, a psychology professor at Davidson Community College in Lexington, North Carolina, and the author of *Perfectionism: What's Bad About Being Too Good*.

Perfectionism tends to make people hide their mistakes, which is what makes it so subversive. Unfortunately, such an approach leaves no means to challenge the idea that value depends on doing flawlessly because it prevents a person from receiving critical feedback that verifies the value of mistakes and affirms self-worth.

Canadian psychologists Gordon L. Flett and Paul L. Hewitt studied the crippling effects of athletes' performance anxiety. They discovered "the perfection paradox," which states that, despite the need for athletes in some sports to achieve ideal performance results, the propensity to be cognitively concerned with   perfect results reduces performance in other ways as well.

A Perfectionist's Signs

The unfavorable effects of your own drive for excellence can be felt by even casual perfectionists (who may not even believe themselves to be perfectionists)... it is not essential for it to reach "Black Swan" levels of perfectionism for it to have a severe influence on your life and health. Perfectionists:

1. **Link their performance with societal acceptance.** They feel that they must be impeccable to be liked or approved (Davis & Cowles, 1991).

2. **Amplify the consequences of their mistakes.** They fear that these errors might lead to catastrophic outcomes (Flett et al., 2002).

3. **Procrastinate a lot.** Their need for perfect conditions before acting can delay progress as they wait for the "right moment" or over-strategize (Steel, 2007).

4. **Adopt an "if...then" belief.** They achieved success, happiness, and peace (Hewitt et al., 2003).

5. **Think 100% is the only metric for success.** Any other result is seen as inadequate or a failure, creating a rigid mindset (Greenspon, 2000).

6. **Judge others harshly.** They try to compensate for self-perceived inadequacies, which is a psychological defense mechanism (Alden et. Al., 1990).

7. **Take on projects only if assured of success.** Or they otherwise avoid them. This binary perspective categorizes outcomes as solely success or failure (Burns, 1980).

8. **Have difficulty trusting others.** Their perfectionism can act as a barrier to genuine connections, as outlined by Brené Brown (2010).

9. **Become defensive when criticized.** A perfectionist may be easy to identify in conversation if they take control by defending themselves against any threat, even when there is none, to preserve their fragile sense of self and how they come across to others (Horney, 1950).

10. **Often feel inadequate.** Because perfection is an unattainable goal, perfectionists frequently feel they aren't quite "there yet." Christina Aguilera, a self-described perfectionist, claims always to strive to surpass herself because she dwells on all the things she has yet to accomplish. The negative emotions of shame, guilt, and anxiety are all strongly connected with maladaptive perfectionism. Underneath it all, perfectionists usually experience guilt and shame as their worst enemies. (Stoeber & Otto, 2006).

11. **Have trouble making decisions.** Perfectionists rarely make decisions because they are so worried about making the wrong choices. If someone is lucky, someone else will decide and take accountability for the outcome. Often, the decision is made automatically (Frost & Shows, 1993).

What Can Help?

The quest for perfection can be difficult since it typically stems from both a desire to do well and a fear of the consequences of performing poorly. This is the perfectionist's double-edged sword.

- ☐ **Put radical self-acceptance into action.** Perfectionists frequently have high standards for other people. We reject what we can't accept as a defence mechanism in others, and the more we focus on our flaws, the more we judge those around us. These intense emotions result from picturing one's ideal self and life; they are a terrifying filter we cannot remove from reality. Being gentle with oneself is necessary if we wish to stop this behavior. With all of our "flaws" and "imperfections," we are considerably less prone to judge others when we accept who we are.

- ☐ **Develop and perform rituals.** There are several things that perfectionists fear. Fear of failure influences all kinds of decisions, such as selecting a partner and starting new projects. As a result, we become unsure and dependent on outside guidance. We must develop the habit of not letting fear control our every action to eliminate such subservient behavior.

- ☐ **Bemoan unfulfilled dreams.** No matter who we are, it's rare to end up becoming the people we imagined ourselves to be when we were five years old. And perfectionists need to accept that. We combat the idea that we are never successful or that we don't matter, so we need to feel confident in ourselves and proud of our achievements constantly. Thus, create a list. As you make a list of your accomplishments from the previous week, month, or year, see how your value emerges on paper.

☐ **Think about how you can be more vulnerable and transparent at work.** Even though it might be challenging, developing your capacity for vulnerability will put you further ahead of the game than trying to be flawless ever could in both your personal and professional lives. Author of *The Gift of Imperfection* and researcher Brené Brown famously said: "Imperfections are not inadequacies; they are reminders that we're all in this together."

☐ **Separate perfectionism from procrastination.** You might become your own worst enemy when procrastination and perfectionism are combined. You may utilize your time wisely and accomplish more without stress if you liberate yourself from this laborious routine. Your concern centers on how failing will affect your self-esteem or how others will see you if you do poorly. Based on your performances, you evaluate your worth and determine whether you succeed or fail. Dichotomous thinking is a component of this contingent-worth anxiety thinking. You are either a winner or a loser in this judging process, deserving or undeserving, strong, or weak. For instance, you aspire for and anticipate at least a B+. The objective is reachable. The anticipation is unwarranted. You feel like a failure after receiving a B.

D. Dealing with Failure

Our capacity to bounce back from adversity and unpleasant experiences is greatly influenced by how we respond to failure, and this in turn has a significant impact on our level of self-mastery.

In our culture, success is not just respected it's expected. It serves as a marker of identity for both individuals and organizations. Contrary to this view, failure is more than just the absence of success; it's an ideological, psychological, and emotional construct that occupies a significant space in our lives. This duality—success and failure—defines us and molds our perceptions of our worth.

We experience failure early in life—first at home, then in primary school—and we quickly see how it could impede our ability to grow academically. For years, students have been terrified of failing tests and assignments since, in the end, our very first failure might determine who we are. Since failure diminishes the value of our efforts at work, our impression of our successes, and our sense of self, we accept the belief that only perfection will do.

Early in the 19th century, the words "breaking in business," "going out of business," and "filing for bankruptcy" were frequently used to describe these events. Over time, references to moral transgressions, material achievement, and personal shortcomings have been incorporated into this purely business idea. How did this change take place? How can a lack of resources cause you to feel unworthy of love and respect?

According to Scott A. Sandler, author of Born Losers: A History of Failure in America, the change in how we view failure is partially a result of how the American dream was viewed in 19th-century America. He says: "Failure is vital for success for the [American] dream, which equates freedom with achievement, to exist and endure. He says that those of us who have failed "embody the American fear that our fondest hopes and worst nightmares may be one and the same." He claims that "it is not enough to achieve. We need failure, the word, and the person...to sort out our own defeats and dreams. Some must fall short."

Why Do People Fail?

The dictionary defines failure as "a lack of success in doing something;" "something you should have done;" and "something not working as it should work." Of the three definitions, the first is more often accepted by society than the others.

Yet, from a statistical point of view, failure is rampant in society. For instance, according to 50 representative compounds that underwent clinical testing between 1993 and 2004, the clinical failure rate for pharmaceuticals undergoing phase II testing in the pharmaceutical industry was reported to be 81%. In another context, major league baseball batters miss the ball 75% of the time (the overall major league baseball batting average for 2020 was 0.253), and we rave about a baseball hitter who bats over 300, meaning they fail 70% of the time.

The null hypothesis, defined as "a speculation or theory based on insufficient evidence that lends itself to further testing and experimentation," is the framework for all well-designed investigations. With further testing, a hypothesis can usually be proven true or false. Of course, the scientific approach includes failure.

The percentage of failed scientific research studies is much higher than generally known but rarely discussed. Regardless of how astute an investigator may have been in hindsight, the scientific method is one of trial and error, even under the best of conditions. Thus, chance must be considered.

The point here is that research in science needs failure to establish valid results, so publishing negative trial results is essential for the scientific enterprise, a fact that had yet to be widely acknowledged by major journals in the past, where primarily positive results were published.

According to Costaca Bradatan, who wrote in the *New York Times,* failure is significant from a wider, more philosophical standpoint for several reasons:

- "Failure allows us to see our existence in its naked condition. Whenever it occurs, failure reveals just how close our existence is to its opposite."

- "Out of our survival instinct or plain sightlessness, we tend to see the world as a solid, reliable, even indestructible place. And we find it extremely difficult to conceive of that world existing without us. We must continue to be inherently flawed, incomplete, erring animals; in other words, there is always a gap between what we are and what we can be. We need to protect, foster, even love this capacity."

☐   "We are designed to fail. The 'existential threat' of that failure has been with us all along, though to survive in a state of relative contentment, most of us have pretended not to see it. No matter how successful our lives turn out to be, no matter how smart, industrious, or diligent we are, the same end awaits us all: "biological failure."

In his book, *Self-Esteem, and Failure in School: Analysis and Policy Implications*, UC Berkeley professor Martin Covington found that students will go through incredible psychological machinations to avoid failure and maintain the sense that they are worthy.

A dysfunctional belief can mean that one is unable and, therefore, not worthy. If a person doesn't believe he or she can succeed — or if repeated failures diminish that belief — then that person will start, consciously or unconsciously, to engage in practices or make excuses to preserve his or her self-worth both in his or her own eyes and in the eyes of others.

The Embarrassment of Failure

The two fundamental motivations for success, the need for achievement and fear of failure, are linked, according to John Atkinson. He argues the need for achievement as "the capacity to feel pride in accomplishment" and fear of failure as "the capacity or propensity to experience shame upon failure."

Research demonstrates that for people with high levels of fear of failure, achievement events are not just chances to learn, improve your competence, or compete against others but are also threatening, judgment-oriented experiences that call into question your entire self-concept. Atkinson argues that shame has been identified as a fear of failure, but until the present research, this proposition had yet to be empirically documented.

Ironically, in doing so, those high in fear of failure keep themselves from the mistakes and failures that many achievement motivation theorists view as the basis for competence development. Shame can be a powerful, painful emotion, so it is unsurprising that individuals high in fear of failure seek to avoid failure. Such individuals often seek to avoid achievement situations in the first place.

The avoidance of failure is thus likely to be a self-perpetuating process in that the very process of avoiding failure is likely to serve a role in maintaining and reinforcing the tendency to avoid failure. In essence, the avoidance of mistakes and failures stunts personal growth which, over time, merely leads to more mistakes and failures.

With the release of her first book, *The Gifts of Imperfection, a New York Times* Best Seller, and the second most watched TED Talk of all time, "The Power of Vulnerability," Brené Brown has served as an ambassador on the global stage for the virtues of vulnerability and imperfection since 2010.

According to Brown, shame is the belief that you will never be successful enough and that you are unlovable and will never fit in because of your flaws and shortcomings. Brown contends that to achieve greatness and lead a happier life, we must embrace who we are and let down our guard, which presents a difficulty because it makes us more prone to failure.

How We Talk About Our Failures

Deep-seated mental biases often influence our perceptions of success and failure. Psychologist Dale T. Miller has highlighted in his research that we readily credit our achievements to internal factors, such as the effort we invest, our inherent skills or our experience, not external influences. Contrarily, a study by Irene Frieze and Bernard Weiner suggests we attribute our failures to external elements.

However, if we fail at a task first, we're less likely to want to help others, according to research by L. Berkowitz and W. H. Connor. However, success at a task followed by positive reinforcement increases our likelihood of being generous and helpful to others, according to research by A. M. Isen.

As Kathryn Schulz points out in her book *Being Wrong*, "the sentence 'I am wrong' describes a logical impossibility. As soon as we know we are wrong, we aren't wrong anymore since recognizing a belief as false is to stop believing it. Thus, we can only say, 'I was wrong.'" She continues that even for those of us who try hard to admit our mistakes, it's almost impossible for us to do so.

Dealing with Failure Successfully

The following is a compilation of suggestions drawn from research and helpful techniques.

1. **Challenge your self-talk.** For instance, a middle-aged writer might think, "Maybe I'm too old to start a writing career" after receiving several rejections. However, if the writer recognized that this was their fixed mindset speaking, they could counter by saying, "Then again, you're never too old to learn a new skill," or "Lots of successful writers started their careers at my age or even later."

2. **Accept "productive failure."** When you give someone a new task with the least amount of guidance possible rather than carefully teaching them how to do it. As Sunita G. Chowrira at the University of British Columbia and her colleagues: "While students often fail to produce satisfactory solutions (hence 'failure'), these attempts help learners encode key features and learn better."

3. **Recognize the difference between doing and being.** Failing at something doesn't make you a failure. Unless you are an exceptional genius when you die, people will remember you for who you were, not for all your achievements. You cannot undo the past, but you can shape your future.

4. **Embrace your emotions with mindfulness.** A variety of uncomfortable emotions, such as embarrassment, anxiety, anger, sadness, and shame accompany failure. Many people will try to avoid these uncomfortable emotions by any means necessary. Observing your emotions and accepting them as they are is part of being mindful.

5. **Have a sense of humor about your failures, and don't take yourself so seriously.** People cope with failures and stress in life in various ways, ranging from distraction to getting social support. But what are the most effective strategies? New research from the University of Kent has revealed that positive reframing, acceptance, and humor are the most effective coping strategies for people dealing with failures.

6. **Be kind to yourself.** Kristin Neff at the University of Texas at Austin is perhaps the most well-known proponent of self-compassion. In 2005, Neff published work finding that students who are self-compassionate in the wake of exam failure go on to study harder for future exams. More recent research has found that being kind to yourself can help you cope with failure.

Summary and Follow-Up

Resilience comes from overcoming hardship; it is not something we are born with, despite some academics' claims to the contrary; however, the skill can be enhanced by using the tips and techniques in this chapter.

7

Personal Productivity

"The key is not to prioritize what's on your schedule, but to schedule your priorities."

– Stephen Covey

Questions to Consider

1. How do you define productivity?

2. What is the difference between productivity and busyness?

3. How do you set and attain goals?

4. How do you eliminate bad habits and acquire good ones?

5. How do you make good decisions?

The ability to plan, create, and produce excellent results for your own endeavors is known as personal productivity. Because of your efforts to reach your goals, stay focused and avoid distractions and counterproductive behaviors, and have a good outlook, self-mastery and personal productivity are closely tied to one another. Personal productivity can be considerably increased by self-mastery, and vice versa. Self-mastery requires the ability to control your time, attention, and focus, as well as your emotions.

A. Productivity

The Elements of Personal Productivity

1. **Focus and concentration.** Concentrating on crucial work while ignoring distractions is a sign of self-mastery. Cal Newport, the author of *Deep Work,* illustrates the significance of uninterrupted concentration.

2. **Goals and objectives.** Setting specific, doable goals is essential for this. Implementing the plan and achieving the goal are both necessary for goal attainment.

3. **Regulation of habits.** This involves using habits to facilitate and bring about the desired outcome. This involves breaking bad habits and creating new good ones.

4. **Self-Motivation.** Those internally motivated to strive toward their goals boost their productivity. Self-motivation and self-control, according to researchers Martin Seligman and Angela Duckworth, are more predictive of successful performance than IQ.

5. **Social skills.** Despite their emphasis on interpersonal connection, according to Daniel Goleman, social skills can indirectly increase productivity since they enhance communication and lessen the likelihood of misunderstandings and conflicts.

6. **Managing time and energy.** This necessitates careful time management, preparation, and, among other things, safeguards against exhaustion and low energy.

7. **Persistence.** People with high levels of personal productivity are persistent in their endeavors, especially when temptations or diversions are present.

8. **Self-reflection.** Self-mastery in productivity requires self-awareness and the ability to reflect on your actions and behaviors. People can identify their areas of strength or need for change, identify negative behaviors, and stop them by engaging in self-reflection.

The Myth of More Hours, More Productivity

You've heard it before: The secret to success is hard work, lots of it. But is that a myth? Surprisingly, a lot of research points the other way. For instance, studies show that successful and wealthy people put in a lot less labor than others who are poor and underpaid.

In an article I published in the *National Post* titled "Willing Slaves Fast Becoming Business Norm," I argued that "Overachieving professionals today are seen as road warriors. They work harder, take on endless additional responsibilities, and earn a lot more than their counterparts in earlier times, and their numbers are growing."

According to the OECD, the average number of full-time Americans work is 47.1 hours per week, which is increasing. The typical workweek in Canada is 40 hours, while it is 35 hours in Europe.

According to authors Sylvia Ann Hewlett and Carolyn Buck Luce of "The Hidden Brain Drain Task Force Report," that appeared in the *Harvard Business Review,* the 40-hour work week is a thing of the past. According to Catherine Ornstein, author *of No Longer Is The American Dream* and *Father Knows Best's Ozzie Nelson, It's Donald Trump, and Survivor in the Office Tower,* workaholism manifests our culture's adoption of an extreme ethos. Friendships and social interactions frequently center on work for professionals. Personal connections are also developed at work; in the past, they were solely made through family, friends, and civic organizations.

The amount of work people undertake has a variety of social effects. Because they place a larger importance on the social fabric, particularly the welfare of children and quality of life, Europeans' opinions toward employment differ significantly from those in North America. Scandinavian countries have pursued a humanization of work agenda that places an emphasis on equal opportunity, childcare, gender parity, and the critical role of the family.

A 2007 survey by Towers Perrin found that only 21% of the nearly 90,000 workers felt fully engaged at work. Almost 40% felt disconnected. According to the Towers Perrin study, businesses with low levels of employee engagement saw a 33% annual decrease in operational income and an 11% annual decline in earnings growth. On the other hand, businesses with high participation levels reported growth in operating income of 19% and in earnings per share of 28%.

The Energy Factor

In a piece for the *Harvard Business Review*, Tony Schwartz, CEO of the Energy Project, and author of *The Way We're Working Isn't Working: The Four Forgotten Needs That Energize Great Performance*, describes how his company, the Energy Project, looked at employee disengagement and work performance ten years ago. In the words of Schwartz, "We believed that burnout was one of its major causes, and we focused almost exclusively on helping people avoid it by managing their energy rather than their time. Time, after all, is finite. However, you can expand your energy and also regularly renew it."

He argues that productivity means "managing energy in all facets of our lives. Emotional depth and resilience depend on active engagement with others and with our own feelings." This argument is made in his earlier book *The Power of Full Engagement: Managing Energy, Not Time, is the Key to High Performance and Personal Renewal*, which he co-wrote with Jim Loehr.

Schwartz claims that the issue goes beyond the number of hours worked and includes what happens to workers' energy levels as well as how they utilize their downtime.

In a survey he conducted, Schwartz found that 60% of respondents had a 20-minute lunch break, and 25% never even left their desks. But various studies, including one by the American Dietetic Association, 75% of office workers, have lunch at their workstations at least two to three days per week.

B. Workaholism and Busyness

Busyness and workaholism have a negative impact on both individual and collective productivity.

Overwork has reportedly become the norm during the past 20 years, particularly in large enterprises. Workaholism is an undetectable addiction in a society that values dedication to one's job. Most of the modern life is spent at work.

However, employers and managers cannot be held solely accountable for the situation. According to Laura Vanderkam, author of *What Most Successful People Do on the Weekend,* many employees lack the self-discipline to draw boundaries between their personal and professional lives. Many people assert that they feel important or in need.

Economists have long argued that putting in extra hours will lower productivity. In the 1930s, British economist John Hicks conducted research on this issue and found that productivity fell as working hours increased. Additionally, John Pencavel of Stanford University has demonstrated in his research that shorter workdays can increase productivity. The study found that productivity dropped when there were no rest days (such as Sundays) and workers put in more than 50 hours per week.

But what traits set apart the most productive employees? The Draugiem Group, a social networking business that makes use of the time-tracking productivity application DeskTime, conducted an experiment to find out. The most effective workers, according to the study's findings, put in less time than anyone else. In fact, they only worked complete eight-hour shifts.

The largest problem we face today, according to famous time usage expert John Robinson, is not "not having enough time," but rather how fragmented, overstimulated, and interrupted our lives are. Gloria Mark, a professor at the University of California, notes that studies have shown that it normally takes 25 minutes to fully resume cognitive attention following an interruption.

The ordinary information worker gets interrupted every three minutes, or around 20 times an hour, according to her research from the

University of California's Information and Computer Sciences, compared to the manager's every eight minutes. Over an eight-hour workday, most of us experience interruptions 50 to 60 times, each lasting five minutes on average. More than four hours out of eight, or 50% of the workday, are full of interruptions.

Multitasking

Research studies show that multitasking is unproductive and significantly lowers productivity. A Stanford University study found multitasking is less efficient than concentrating on one thing at a time. The researchers also found that people consistently exposed to many electronic information streams are less able to pay attention, remember details, or switch between tasks than people who concentrate on one item at a time.

According to University of London studies, those who multitask while completing cognitive activities have an IQ loss comparable to what would occur if they had consumed marijuana or stayed up all night.

Here are Some Suggestions to Help You Become More Productive

- ☐ **Embrace quiet moments.** There is evidence to support the idea that being calm and unoccupied can boost your vigor and creativity.

- ☐ **Learn to say "no."** Making time sacrifices for others is usually expected in workplace settings, whether it is through mentorship or keeping an open-door policy. Often, the productivity improvements others make come at a cost to you.

- ☐ **Stop gauging your worth in terms of your achievements.** According to the most recent studies, simply evaluating your development benefits your sense of accomplishment and how knowledgeable and effective you feel at work. *The Progress Principle's* originator, Teresa Amabile, prefers progress—moving your work forward—to productivity—getting things done properly and efficiently, regardless of their relevance.

☐ **Schedule breaks during your workday.** Every 52 minutes or less, you should take a 17-minute rest.

☐ **Schedule tasks using your calendar rather than a to-do list.** Scheduling also has the added advantage of making you accountable for your duties rather than keeping them hidden on a covert to-do list.

☐ **Take frequent vacations or sabbaticals.** Skipping vacation days is a bad idea since it reduces productivity and harms the economy.

☐ **Allocate two to two and a half hours per day for maximum output**. *The 7 Hour Workweek* author Tim Ferris suggests avoiding checking email during the first hour or two of the day.

☐ **Form efficient email habits.** According to research from the University of California, Irvine and the US Army, people who don't check their email frequently at work are less stressed and more productive than those who do. Up to 30% of the workday can be spent responding to emails throughout the day.

☐ **Manage and minimize interruptions.** This is a logical development of the preceding idea, and it involves scheduling alone, peaceful time to complete your tasks and objectives.

☐ **Give up multi-tasking.** Being more productive requires developing your ability to concentrate, as only a very tiny percentage of people can efficiently work on multiple tasks at once.

The "Busyness" Epidemic

Busyness is all about a focus and even obsession with mastering your internal world. It would not make sense to think of being busy and rushing through an examination of your internal world for mastery, which should be calm, slow, and reflective.

When you're busy, it's easy to feel overburdened, overwhelmed, snowed under, swamped, confined, and under pressure because you think there isn't enough time to complete everything you've committed to or want to do.

U.S.A. Today, the findings of a multi-year survey in 2018 were published to examine how people felt about time and their personal workload. Unsurprisingly, women reported being busier than males, and those between 30 and 60 were the busiest. It was discovered that since 1987, people have reported being busier than the year before, with 69% stating they were either "busy" or "very busy" and only 8% claiming they were "not very busy."

Psychiatrist and head of the Johns Hopkins Hospital's Anxiety Disorders Clinic Joseph Bienvenu treats people who are so overscheduled that they cannot sleep, think clearly, or find time for essential activities like exercise. According to him, emotional pain brought on by busyness shows up as impatience and anger, difficulties focusing, and problems regulating emotions.

Celebrities routinely complain about "having no life" or "needing a vacation" on Twitter, and a review of holiday letters reveals a sharp rise in allusions to "crazy schedules" since the 1960s.

Advertising, which is frequently a barometer of social norms, used to show rich people relaxing by the pool or on a yacht; nowadays, those ads are being replaced by ones that show busy people who work hard and have little free time, as in Cadillac's Super Bowl commercial, which featured a busy and leisure-deprived businessman making fun of people who take long vacations.

In a *Boston Globe* article, Susan Koven, an internal medicine specialist at Massachusetts General Hospital, claimed that she had observed "a sort of epidemic" in which patients were all having the same issue, which included fatigue, irritability, insomnia, anxiety, headaches, heartburn, bowel disturbances, back pain, and weight gain.

Tim Kreider makes the case that if you live in America in the twenty-first century, you've undoubtedly had to listen to many people talk about how busy they are in his piece "The Busy Trap" in the *New York Times*. He asserts that this is frequently a brag that is "disguised as a complaint," but these same folks frequently express complaints about being drained and dead tired.

According to Dr. Christiane Northup, a women's health expert and *New York Times* best-selling author, our culture greatly values being excessively busy. She wrote, "We are conditioned to think that being busy means we are good, worthy, and successful."

Even children these days have too much going on. Today's adolescents and teens are overworked, overburdened, and pressured to a degree that was previously only found in juvenile mental patients, claims Jean Twenge, a psychology professor at San Diego State University. Statistics show that 75% of parents claim to be too busy to read to their children at night. A growing number of kids are enrolled in daycare and endless after-school activities.

You can't just decide to stop doing everything that's expected of you as a man, a woman, a parent, or an employee one morning. Of course, the problem is that we create standards for a busy life as a culture rather than as individuals. Even worse, the system is rigged because the standards keep rising. People will send you more emails if you try to keep up with them.

A Plan for Dealing with Busyness and Being More Productive

So, how should one manage their hectic schedule? The following suggestions are made:

☐ **Stop bragging about your busyness.** Quit reminding yourself and others how busy you are. Along with seeming arrogant, you also fool yourself into thinking you have no influence over the situation.

- ☐ **Reduce your to-do list by 50%.** Distinguish between what is "important" and what is "urgent," which is usually the urgency of another person.

- ☐ **Establish procedures or a strategy to handle interruptions.** Peak work times should occur without interruptions of any kind.

- ☐ **Avoid multitasking.** People who are successful focus on one thing at a time.

- ☐ **Get strong at saying "no" repeatedly.** To everyone, and once is not enough.

- ☐ **Throughout each day, take numerous short breaks.** Don't wait for a big, long break.

- ☐ **Re-evaluate your priorities and focus your efforts there.** Important and urgent combined should come before anything else.

- ☐ **Having fewer possessions can make your life easier.** Declutter and minimize.

- ☐ **Spend a lot of time by yourself.** Time in nature is crucial.

- ☐ **Develop good habits and eliminate bad ones.** Have a habit routine.

- ☐ **Significantly scale back the number of activities you commit to,** and refrain from beginning new ones before finishing existing ones. For everything new you take on, eliminate one thing you are presently doing.

- ☐ **Quit indulging in FOMO (Fear of Missing Out).** Stop comparisons with others.

- ☐ **Reduce the number of decisions you must make.** Too many choices and too much information can overload our cognitive abilities.

C. Setting Goals and Habits

Goals

At the end of each year, most of us reflect on our short—and long—term goals. It all comes down to having the right questions to ask yourself—questions that allow goal setting to provide more purpose and maximize accomplishment and achievement.

Here are 10 good questions to ask yourself to help you set goals:

1. **"What are possible pitfalls?"** What dangers exist that could keep you from reaching your objectives? What has sidetracked you before?

2. **"What regrets prevent you from making wise goals?"** You don't want to look back ten years (or even one year) from now feeling like you lived someone else's story. According to author and former palliative nurse Bronnie Ware, the top regret of the dying is "How can I live a life true to myself and my values, and not the life others expect of me."

3. **"What practices will help you achieve your goals?"** The question "How can I work on my life, not just in it?" urges proactivity rather than constant reacting. Recommitting to the idea of challenge, enjoying the thrill of learning new talents, and getting closer to your ideal self are all important aspects of this process.

4. **"Are you establishing reasonable objectives that are neither overly complex nor underly simple?"** You can set higher standards for your achievements and the joy you provide to the world by asking yourself, "What's the difference between a good and great next year or decade?" Also, think about this: The answer to the question, "If I knew I couldn't fail, what would I try?" frequently contains the secret to greatness.

5. **"What are my superpowers, and how will I use them for good?"** Consider setting a goal that does good for others or the world.

6. **"What goals would make you happy or feel fulfilled?"** Reflect to consider what your happiest moments in life have been. Goal planning should be about satisfaction and happiness, not only achievements or task completion.

7. **"Whose needs shall I have satisfied?"** Set yourself up to help others with the goals you set. When you look back one or ten years from now, who will you have helped with your time and energy? It's easy to become overly self-centered when making objectives, but true satisfaction comes from knowing you made a difference in other people's lives.

Which Is More Important, Goals or Habits?

Recently, some have pushed people to focus on habits rather than goals when they wish to accomplish anything in life or at business. Typically, the advice given is to establish and carry out an objective.

Which one is true? The answer is "both." But we tend to mistakenly favor goals over habits.

The Argument for Goals

We've all heard it before: "Set lofty goals if you want to accomplish anything significant," and it's said by CEOs, management consultants, self-help gurus, personal coaches, and managers.

Despite the frequent use of "stretch goals" or "hairy audacious goals" as motivational and performance management methods, there is some evidence that goal setting may be useless, if not a waste of time.

We associate goals and objectives with success; in our culture, a person or organization can only be regarded as successful once goals are accomplished. To accomplish this leaders frequently use a continuous focus on "improvement," "bigger and better," through more and more effort, and higher productivity. Our society is preoccupied with goal setting, especially "stretch" or "audacious" ambitions, both on an individual level and in companies.

According to conventional wisdom, we should set our goals in the following order:

- ☐ Describe the overall result you anticipate.

- ☐ Set definite, specific goals.

- ☐ Be clear about the measures you'll use to gauge goal success.

- ☐ Define clear goals, objectives, strategies, methods, and deadlines.

- ☐ Describe goals in terms of specific outcomes or repercussions.

- ☐ Describe the expected benefits for achieving your goal successfully as well as the next steps you'll take if you don't.

The Myth of Successful Goal-Setting

Both scholarly and research-based sources and well-known self-help sources are considered to promote the significance of goal setting. As an illustration, barely 3% of Yale University's graduating seniors from the class of 1953 stated that they had written goals for the future. Only 7% of the class's surviving members reported having written goals for the future when researchers checked in with them 20 years later.

There is a popular belief that goal success is only possible if you write them down, based upon a supposed research study conducted at Yale University.

All Yale researchers and graduates of the class of 1953 assert that they never carried out or participated in such a study.

Also, I need to find a study that I am aware of shows a connection between visualizing objectives and achieving them, despite the advice of self-help books like *The Secret,* which exhorts readers to set big goals by using visualization.

Though the goal-setter is frequently held responsible, the underlying problem may lie in the effectiveness of goal-setting. Despite the widespread use of goal setting, there is overwhelming evidence that despite best efforts and intentions, individuals and organizations consistently need to consistently accomplish their goals.

Setting Ambitious or "Stretch" Goals Has Drawbacks

Aubrey Daniels believes that stretch goals could be a better management tactic. The author of *Oops! In his article 13 Management Practices That Waste Time and Money,* Daniels cites studies demonstrating how people's performance declines when they regularly fall short of stretch goals. In another survey, he found that 10% of workers had met stretch goals. According to Daniels, people are only motivated by goals when they have previously achieved them and received positive feedback and incentives.

The Center for Disease Control estimate that 34% of Americans are overweight and another 34% are obese, meaning that over 70% of the population's health is precarious. This is true despite the growth of weight-loss programs, which primarily focus on weight-loss goals. The straightforward explanation would be to attribute someone's lack of effort or willpower; however, the issue could be with the viability of goal setting.

Paradoxically, firms that can least afford the risks connected with them find stretch goals to be the most alluring. Stretch goals were studied by Sim Sitkin and colleagues, who then reported their findings in the *Harvard Business Review.* They discovered that the organizations most inclined to pursue them were desperate, troubled ones that would find it difficult to change if the goals weren't met.

In the book *The Hazards of Goal Pursuit* is a book by Laura A. King and Chad M. King said: "Empirical evidence that reveals the negative aspects of goals in human life."

Goal setting, in the opinion of Adam Galinsky, a professor at Northwestern University's Kellogg School of Management and one of the authors of a Harvard Business School report titled "Goals Gone Wild", "has been treated like an over-the-counter medication when it should be treated with more care, as a prescription-strength mediation."

According to the authors of "Goals Gone Wild," defining goals has several negative effects, including "an overly narrow focus that neglects non-goal areas; a rise in unethical behavior; distorted risk preferences; corrosion of organizational culture; and reduced intrinsic motivation."

Lisa Ordonez of the University of Arizona and Maurice Schweitzer of the University of Pennsylvania are the co-authors of "Goals Gone Wild" and have researched the psychology of goal achievement. According to their research, a sizable percentage of persons who self-report achieving their goals lie to make up the gap if they were only partially successful.

Recent neuroscience studies have demonstrated that the brain functions defensively and resists change. Therefore, any goals requiring considerable behavioral, or thought-pattern change would inevitably be met with resistance. The brain is designed to seek benefits and avoid unpleasant feelings, including dread. When the goal-setter begins to harbor a fear of failing, it becomes a "demotivator," making the goal-setter want to revert to past behaviors.

According to new research published in the INFORMS journal *Organization Science,* stretch goals have a negative impact on performance for many businesses. The study was carried out by John Sterman of the Sloan School of Management at MIT, Miles Yang of Curtin University, Philip Yetton of Deakin University, and Michael Shayne Gary of UNSW Business School in Sydney.

According to the authors, "increased performance for a few participants compared to moderate goals, but many participants abandoned the stretch goals in favor of lower self-set goals or adopted a survival goal when faced with the prospect of bankruptcy, the researchers revealed. Stretch goals led to greater performance variance across organizations, and substantial performance gaps that prompted additional risk-taking were typically not reached."

Habits

In his book, *The Power of Habit: Why We Do What We Do in Life and Business*, Charles Duhigg, a business reporter for *The New York Times*, details how certain companies have had great success by changing people's habits. These companies have been using the "habit loop," a powerful psychological pattern, intentionally or by mistake.

The cue, which Duhigg describes as "sort of a trigger for an automatic behavior to start unfolding," the routine, which is the behavior itself, and the reward "tells our brain whether we should store this habit for future use or not," are the three stages that make up the habit loop.

According to Duhigg, changing people or entire organizations may be accomplished using the science of habit formation. To achieve this, you must concentrate on a specific action he terms a "keystone habit." "If you can change a keystone habit, you unlock all these other patterns in some of your life or an organization," asserts Duhigg.

The cue, craving, response, and reward are the additional four components James Clear added to Duhigg's habit loop in his best-selling book *Atomic Habits*. The cue causes a craving, which inspires a reaction, delivers a reward, and satisfies the craving, and then the response and reward become connected with the cue.

A regular practice or routine known as an atomic habit, which is a component of the system of compound growth, is not only quick and easy to carry out but also a source of extraordinary power. Clear explains:

☐ Repeated bad behaviors don't occur because you don't want to change; rather, they do so because your mechanism for change is ineffective.

☐ Even though adjustments at first seem inconsequential and little, they will compound into incredible benefits if you're willing to stick with them for years.

☐ Habits are the self-improvement version of compound interest.

☐ The best way to change your behaviors is to concentrate on who you want to become rather than what you want to achieve.

☐ The four fundamental laws of behavior change—make it obvious, make it beautiful, make it simple, and make it rewarding—can be used to help us develop better habits.

☐ Human behavior is influenced indirectly by the environment.

How Habits and Goals Relate

In his book *Atomic Habits,* James Clear provides a method for forming positive habits and evicting unfavorable ones:

1. Rather than focusing on setting goals, create positive habits and processes. Habits are involuntarily acquired set ways of thinking, feeling, or doing that are learned through earlier experience and repeated over time. On the other hand, achieving consistent, long-term behavior can be hindered by goals.

2. Small behaviors can make a big difference. Clear exemplifies how making incremental progress each day is crucial for the development of habits. He asserts that, although small, daily improvements of even 1% can add up to a 37% improvement over the course of a year. In comparison, if you improve by 1% less every day for a year, your improvement will be extremely close to zero.

3. Recognize and use a habit system that consists of four steps: 1) trigger, or what kicks off your habit; 2) yearning, or the motivation behind every habit; 3) reaction, or the habit you'll really do; and 4) reward, or what satisfies the craving or teaches us.

4. The four laws of behavior change—make it obvious, attractive, easy, and gratifying—would be the antithesis of breaking a bad habit.

5. Use habit stacking, which involves introducing a new habit after each productive one. For example, I might meditate for ten minutes after drinking my coffee in the morning before going over my to-do list from the previous evening.

6. Find a reliable accountability partner who can assist you in tracking the growth of your habit and provide encouragement and candid feedback.

Additional Practices to Boost Productivity

According to Charles Duhigg, "Keystone Habits" are modest steps or behaviors that can trigger a domino effect into other parts of our lives or enterprises. He asserts that keystone habits "can affect how people work, eat, live, spend, and communicate" and that success "...doesn't depend on getting every single thing right, but instead relies on identify the keystone habits that will help you achieve your goals."

According to behavior change specialists, you should concentrate on changing a very small number of habits at once. B.J. Fogg of Stanford University made the proposal that you should aim to change no more than three behaviors at once. For the record, Dr. Fogg is referring to very specific habits. For example, losing 10 pounds in 90 days would be more specific than just "lose weight".

Decrease decision-making because it can impede the formation of wholesome behaviors. In a study published in the *Journal of Personality and Social Psychology*, participants demonstrated decreased self-control, including decreased physical stamina, decreased persistence in the face of failure, and increased procrastination, after making several decisions about the kinds of products to buy.

Monitor your behavior. Keep a record of how frequently you practice any habit. Mark each time you finish or practice the new behavior in a small notebook, in your phone's notes app, or on a calendar. Keep a record of the times you skipped or neglected to practice the habit as well.

Perfectionism can seriously impede your ability to achieve your goals and build healthy routines and be a factor in deteriorating or subpar performance and demotivation. According to clinical psychologist Jessamy Hibberd, "Study after study demonstrates that self-criticism leads to a decline in performance and demotivation. Self-criticism is the biggest obstacle to new habits."

D. Decision-Making

According to some online sources, an adult makes over 35,000 conscious decisions daily; however, Cornell University researchers discovered that we make about 200 decisions alone each week solely about our diet.

As a result, decision-making has been researched in several academic disciplines, including math, sociology, psychology, economics, and political science.

People typically highlight qualities like honesty, friendliness, humor, courage, or other virtues when asked to list their greatest assets. Surprisingly, of the virtues that a study with over 1 million individuals looked at, self-control or willpower came in dead last. According to Florida State University social scientist Roy F. Baumeister, willpower influences all our decisions.

According to Baumeister, the most successful people don't have particularly strong willpower while making decisions; instead, they conserve their willpower by establishing routines and habits, reducing their stress. According to a suggestion made in an article by Harvard cognitive scientist Steven Pinker, these people utilize their self-control or willpower to avoid crises rather than to get through them.

Effective, conscious decision-making requires cognitive resources, and because increasingly complex decisions put a strain on these resources, the quality of our decisions declines as decision complexity increases, according to research by Ap Kigksterhuis, Maarten Bos, Loran Nordgen, and Rick van Baaren, published in the esteemed journal *Science*.

According to Prince Ghuman and Matt Johnson in their book *Blindsight: The (Mostly) Hidden Ways Marketing Reshapes Our Brains*, "When it comes to making decisions, our brain functions in two modes. One mode is largely automatic, it makes reactive decisions based on intuition. The second mode is deliberate, it makes rational, analytical decisions. However, the second mode is finite, meaning "we can only make so many logical decisions," they write.

To find out what happens when people's decision-making abilities are overworked, Angelika Dimoka, Director of The Centre for Neural Decision-Making at Temple University, conducted studies that were published in the journal *Neuroimage*. She discovered logical and rational prefrontal cortex functioning declines when it becomes overloaded with information, and as a result, subjects in her experiments started to make stupid mistakes and bad decisions.

So much for the idea of making well-informed decisions, Sheena Iyengar of Columbia University and author of *The Art of Choosing* studied the effects of more information for people making investment decisions and concluded that too many choices or too much information did not make for better decisions.

She continues, "Instead of making better choices, we become overwhelmed by choice, sometimes even afraid of it. Choice no longer offers opportunities but imposes constraints. It's not a marker of liberation but of suffocation by meaningless minutiae. We all have physical, mental, and emotional limitations that make it impossible for us to process every piece of information."

The Role of Emotions in Decision-Making

Neuroscientists Daeyeol Lee of Yale University, Daniel Salzman of

Columbia University, and Xiao-Jing Wang of Yale University have discovered the following conclusions concerning decision-making:

☐ Our emotions influence all our decisions.

☐ We consider incentives or rewards in most of our decisions.

☐ Improper brain function and negative emotional states, such as severe anxiety, negatively influence decision-making.

Anil Seth's book, *30-Second Brain*, describes how Antonio Damasio's patient, "Elliott," a once-successful businessman, underwent neurosurgery for a tumor and lost a part of his brain—the orbitofrontal cortex—that connects the frontal lobes with the emotions. He could no longer make decisions—even the simplest ones.

To explain how visceral emotion affects human behavior, Damasio later developed the somatic marker hypothesis. For instance, in a card game, he showed that people's fingers begin to perspire before picking up from a losing pile, even before they are aware of their poor judgment.

Daniel Kahneman and Amos Tversky demonstrated that the emotional impact of losses is twice as powerful as the emotional impact of wins, which impacts our decision-making in predictable ways. For instance, it explains our stubborn inability to write off bad investments.

Can You Make Decisions Based on Gut Feelings?

The question of whether our leaders—or any of us, for that matter—trust our brains and rational thinking when making important decisions or whether we make better decisions based on our gut instincts and emotions has been raised by recent research on the process of decision-making, which has revealed surprising results that defy conventional wisdom.

When asked, "When should you trust your gut?," psychologist and Nobel Prize winner in economics Daniel Kahneman and senior scientist at MacroCognition Gary Klein conducted study on using intuition to support decision-making under duress. "Never," Klein retorted, adding that executives should actively and purposefully assess their gut instincts.

According to a study by Joseph Mikels, Sam Maglio, Andrew Reed, and Lee Kaplowitz that appeared in the journal *Emotion*, gut instincts are effective at making quick decisions. The researchers gave respondents a series of complex decisions of various types and asked them to trust their gut instinct or reason it out with knowledge. Overall, they found that using your gut led to considerably superior results than trying to sort out the nuances.

Decision-Making with Mindfulness

The findings of the Wharton School of Business study were released in the 2013 issue of *Psychological Science* and demonstrated how 15 minutes of mindfulness meditation might improve decision-making.

Researchers discovered that a brief mindfulness practice helped people make more logical decisions by considering the information at hand in the present, which resulted in more positive results in the future. The study's principal investigator Andrew Hafenbrack found that mindfulness can improve decision-making by thwarting ingrained inclinations.

Making mindful decisions can stop compulsive or addictive behavior patterns and lead you along a route that benefits your long-term health, happiness, and general well-being.

Brain-Gut Connection

Recent research published by academics and neuroscientists shows a clear connection between the gut and the brain.

Dr. Linda Rinaman of Florida State University describes how the brain and gut are constantly communicating via the vagus nerve, which runs from the gut to the brain. Rinaman claims that gut-to-brain signals have a "powerful influence on emotions, mood, and decisions and are often a response to worrisome or threatening stimuli and events."

Researchers Rinaman and James Maniscalco from the University of Illinois at Chicago claim that vagal feedback signals are highly protective and promote cautious. "Vagal feedback signals can serve as a warning signal to assist us in stopping ourselves from making risky or unwise decisions."

According to Rinaman, a high-fat diet can produce an inflammatory reaction in the GI tract, transmitting signals via the vagus nerve and resulting in sensations of anxiety and sadness. She also claims that our eating habits might occasionally cause changes in behavior or mental state and greatly impact how well our stomach communicates with our brain.

Considering how much data is coming at us at any given minute— over 200 billion emails will be written and received daily this year alone— there may be some justification for controlling the fire hose of information that threatens to overwhelm our brains with useless information.

Joel Pearson, an associate professor of psychology at the University of New South Wales in Australia, found evidence that people can use their intuition or gut feelings to make decisions that are better, faster, more accurate, and more confident in a study that was published in the journal *Psychological Science.*

What Characterizes a Good Decision?

Consensus-seeking should never be your objective, but this does not grant you the right to take unilateral action. Great decisions are shaped by considering a wide range of perspectives. Consult with those who can make a substantial contribution if you want to make an informed selection. This does not imply that you should investigate every viewpoint. The appropriate individuals must clearly express their viewpoints and possess the necessary competence to assist the responsible decision-maker.

A scourge that afflicts people's decision-making frameworks is short-termism. Focusing just on immediate results can be tempting, especially if your performance is only evaluated on how well you do your annual task. Great choices strike a balance between immediate and long-term benefits. Consider the short-term vs. long-term expenses and advantages as you weigh risk vs. effect.

Habits to Help You Make Better Decisions

- ☐ **Watch out for overconfidence, as it can swiftly result in bad decision-making.** Studies consistently demonstrate that people tend to exaggerate both their performance and the accuracy of their knowledge. Comfort comes from familiarity and overconfidence, and there's a good chance you'll make some poor decisions since you've grown accustomed to your routines and need to be made aware of the risk or damage you're causing.

- ☐ **Evaluate the risks associated with every action.** The facts are the same in both cases, but research shows that people who hear "10% of people die" perceive their risk of failure to be higher. For example, take two surgeons who tell their patients, "Ninety percent of people who undergo this procedure live," and the other surgeon who says, "Ten percent of people who undergo this procedure die."

- ☐ **Put the problem to rest.** You could take a lot of time analyzing the benefits and drawbacks, as well as the possible risks and rewards when faced with a challenging decision, such as whether to relocate to a new place or change occupations. Additionally, data demonstrates that considering all your options has many benefits, but doing so excessively might be harmful.

- ☐ **Make it a daily ritual to reflect on your choices for the day.** When one of your decisions doesn't turn out nicely, consider what went wrong. Consider the lessons you can learn from every error you make. Set aside time to think back on your errors, whether you forgot your umbrella at home and got soaked on the way to work or broke your budget because you couldn't resist an impulsive buy.

☐ **Identify your shortcuts.** You're biased in some respects, though admitting it can be awkward. It's hard to be entirely unbiased. In truth, your brain has developed heuristics, or mental shortcuts, to help you make judgments more quickly. These mental shortcuts might lead you astray even though they spare you from spending hours agonizing over every decision you make. Consider the mental shortcuts that result in poor decisions on a regular basis. You might be able to become a little more objective if you admit the false assumptions you may have about people or circumstances.

☐ **Take the opposing view.** You're likely to hold onto a belief after you've decided it is true. It relates to the psychological concept of belief perseverance. There's a strong probability you've formed some views that don't work for you, and it takes more convincing evidence to change a belief than it did to form it. For instance, you might shy away from speaking up in meetings because you think you're a poor public speaker. Or perhaps you quit going on dates because you think you are lousy at relationships. Additionally, you've formed opinions regarding specific racial or ethnic groupings. These ideas that you assume are always true or 100% correct might lead you wrong, such as "People who work out a lot are narcissists" or "Rich people are evil." Arguing against your views is the most effective approach to refute them. Discuss all the benefits of speaking up in a meeting if you're not sure you should. Or, if you're of the opinion that the wealthy are terrible, give examples of how wealthy individuals may be helpful or nice.

☐ **Speak to yourself like you would a reliable friend.** You'll probably find the solution comes to you more readily when you're visualizing yourself offering advice to someone else when you ask yourself, "What would I say to a friend who had this problem?"

☐ **Establish a due date for yourself.** Setting a deadline, according to Levy, "allows us to advance rather than remain immobilized in the worry of making the "wrong" choice." The best method to give yourself a deadline is to establish a date for your final decision so you have time to consider the benefits and cons and sit with your feelings. It can be a good way to avoid decision paralysis.

☐ **Be mindful of your three brains.** We all have three, not just you. The best brain for reasoning, rational decision-making, creativity, and empathy is your cephalic (head) brain. You can find passion, compassion, and values in your cardiac (heart) brain. Courage, self-defence, and your authentic self are in your enteric (gut) brain. All three heads should be heard. Which one should be the deciding factor here?

☐ **Apply the rule of ten.** Before making a choice, consider where you'll be in 10 days, 10 weeks, 10 months, and 10 years from now. Then, consider how you will feel after making this choice.

☐ **Consider your biases.** While leaders must use their instincts, they must also critically examine themselves and understand that often "acting on your gut" sometimes means being influenced by your own biases.

☐ **When making decisions, use your values as a compass and a filter.** When presented with a difficult decision, ask yourself, "Is my decision consistent with my values? My ethical and moral beliefs?" and "How will this enhance my life?"

Summary and Further Follow-Up

Examples of managing personal productivity on both an internal and external level include controlling perfectionism, procrastination, focus and attention, self-motivation and emotion regulation, controlling interruptions and multitasking, learning how to set and achieve goals, establishing good habits, and safeguarding your time and energy.

8

Moral Choices

"Always do what is right. It will gratify half of mankind and astound the other half."

– Mark Twain

Questions to Consider:

1. How do morality and ethics impact our ability for self-mastery?

2. What is meant by moral choices and how does it impact self-mastery?

3. What are the elements of moral choices?

4. What are the benefits of making moral choices?

5. How do morality and ethics help you make good decisions?

Making good choices, especially when it comes to doing the right thing, is a crucial part of personal growth and self-mastery. This kind of alignment can give us a sense of purpose, help us make better decisions, and enhance our integrity.

Famous thinkers have long emphasized the importance of making good choices. Aristotle suggested that living a moral life leads to a state of well-being and happiness or "eudaimonia."

On a similar note, renowned psychologist Laurence Kohlberg developed a theory suggesting that we evolve through stages of moral thought by consistently making good choices.

The Swiss psychologist Jean Piaget likewise emphasized the significance of moral choices in the maturation of morality and intellect.

Piaget believed that by making choices and considering the consequences, people develop a sense of right and wrong, a sense of justice, and autonomy over their own activities. This active decision-making and introspective process leads to self-mastery.

Viktor Frankl, an Austrian psychiatrist and survivor of the Holocaust, emphasized the importance of moral judgments in defining meaning and purpose in life. According to Frankl, people can achieve self-mastery and a sense of fulfillment by consciously living in line with their ideals, even in challenging circumstances.

According to developmental psychologist Robert Kegan, moral judgments are essential to the stages of development known as self-authoring and self-transformation. During these stages, individuals take responsibility for their choices and critically assess their beliefs and moral standards, considering their self-established ideals. This process of moral agency and self-authorship must be experienced to develop self-mastery.

In his book *The Happiness Hypothesis,* social psychologist Jonathan Haidt argues that upholding your moral standards promotes psychological well-being and a sense of fulfillment.

William Damon, a well-known psychologist and an authority on moral development, argues in his book, *The Path to Purpose,* that making moral decisions and living up to your principles and goals are essential to finding your purpose in life and provide a framework for personal mastery.

The Elements of Moral Choices

- ☐ **Moral standards and values.** Moral ideals and principles are fundamental rules or norms that are the basis for making moral choices. Decency, justice, fairness, beneficence, and non-maleficence are a few examples of these.

- ☐ **Outcomes.** The potential outcomes or impacts of a choice significantly impact moral decisions. For instance, utilitarianism emphasizes maximizing happiness or usefulness for the greatest number of individuals. This approach relies a decision's moral significance on the consequences. As an illustration, someone might donate money to a charity because they believe it will benefit others. Where utilitarianism presents difficulty is when the decision or choice to be made is highly personal. For example, the ethicist's trolley choice, where a trolley with broken brakes can proceed down one of two tracks, where on one track is someone you love (e.g., wife or husband), and on the other track a family of 4 unknown to you. Your choice would impact who dies.

☐ **Intentions.** The intentions underlying an action are taken into consideration while making moral judgments. Immanuel Kant, a German philosopher, advanced theories prioritizing an action's intrinsic moral virtues regardless of the outcomes. This viewpoint emphasizes the importance of an action's motivations. For instance, someone may be honest because they believe it is valuable, whether it yields favorable results or not.

☐ **Moral evaluation.** Steps in moral reasoning include critically evaluating the options offered and considering the ethical implications of each choice. It might be required for this to analyze the relevant moral principles, the expected results, and the motivations behind each action. People's moral reasoning is influenced by their values, cultural norms, and life experiences.

☐ **Context.** The circumstances under which a moral choice is made can significantly impact our decisions. Relativism recognizes that moral standards can vary between environments and cultures. In contrast to the moral and legal prohibitions against killing people, killing is not only permitted but even encouraged during times of conflict and war.

☐ **Empathy and compassion.** A person's ability to understand, relate to, and support others in their experiences—which might affect their moral judgments—is a component of their capacity for empathy and compassion. Empathy for others makes us more likely to consider their needs and take steps to promote kindness and justice. When we are compassionate, we are more likely to take action to help others.

The Benefits and Effects of Moral Decisions

Making moral choices has various benefits and can be advantageous to both individuals and society at large. It involves making moral judgments that align with moral principles and conventions rather than out of necessity or self-interest.

Having a moral basis for decisions in life entails more than referring to established religions, though they can be a source of guidance. The reasons behind those decisions are described in the following:

1. **Inner integrity.** People's feeling of personal integrity is bolstered by making moral decisions that allow them to live out their ideals and principles. When our actions are in line with our values and beliefs, we feel better about ourselves, more secure in who we are, and more capable of controlling our lives.

2. **Building trust.** Making moral choices fosters relationships and establishes trust. Integrity and moral conduct can build connections, foster trust, and help one build a good reputation.

3. **Promoting justice and fairness.** Making moral decisions typically involves keeping justice and fairness in mind, which produces equitable consequences. By prioritizing these concepts, people can encourage fairness and a more just and equal society.

4. **Personal growth**. Making moral choices can advance personal growth. By considering ethical dilemmas and choosing actions that are consistent with our beliefs, we can increase our capacity for self-awareness, empathy, and moral reasoning, which ultimately leads to self-mastery.

5. **Encouraging moral behavior and good character.** Making moral choices helps people develop an ethical personality and improve their good deeds.

6. **Finding purpose.** Making moral choices can help us identify our purpose in life and give both our personal and professional lives significance.

Living a Life with Purpose

Imagine waking up every day with a clear sense of why you are here on earth and what you're meant to do. That's living with purpose. It's that internal compass that provides direction and meaning to life. And while it might seem abstract, it's grounded in the choices we make and the values we hold dear.

Is the Purposeful Life the Same as a Happy One?

This age-old question has been pondered by philosophers, scientists and spiritual leaders alike. Some find happiness in fleeting moments, while others see it as a byproduct of a life full of meaning.

Consider the human rights advocate who, to find fulfillment, is imprisoned while fighting for justice. Does being gregarious and spending their nights (and perhaps days) hopping from party-to-party matter and increase their quality of life?

These queries go beyond the realm of academia. They can assist us in deciding where to focus our time and effort so that we can live the lives we want.

Sometimes, the phrases "happiness" and "subjective well-being" are used synonymously. To assess a person's subjective well-being, questions concerning their level of life satisfaction (evaluative), a tendency to experience both positive and negative emotions (affective), and sense of meaning and purpose (eudemonic) are frequently asked.

In her 2007 book *The How of Happiness*, Sonja Lyubomirsky, a researcher in positive psychology, defined happiness as "the experience of joy, contentment, or positive well-being, linked with a sense that your life is good, significant, and valuable."

A feeling of significance or purpose is what is meant by the term of "meaning," which includes questions like "Why are we here?" and "What is my life's purpose?" Because they discuss the importance of living or existence in general, are applicable.

Life's meaning and purpose share common boundaries; more specifically, it's believed that living a meaningful life depends on a variety of elements, some of which include having a purpose in life or forming habits that are inspired by one.

However, professionals have debated on what "happy" is and how to evaluate it, just like everyone else.

Others link happiness to ephemeral emotional sensations or even peaks in brain activity in the pleasure centers. These aspects of happiness have been lumped together by some studies under the general heading of "subjective well-being," which also includes assessments of both happy and negative emotions and overall life satisfaction.

The statement that "a happy life and a meaningful life have certain differences" is supported by a study Roy Baumeister co-authored with academics from Stanford University and the University of Minnesota and published in *the Journal of Positive Psychology.*

In a study involving 397 adults, Baumeister and his colleagues looked at the links between respondents' levels of life satisfaction and meaning and various behavioral, mood, relationship, health, stress, careers, and other activities.

They were interested in learning more about the differences between the two and learned that having a purpose in life and being happy are not always mutually exclusive. Their statistical analysis sought to distinguish between factors that contributed to meaning but not happiness in life and factors that contributed to meaning but not happiness in life.

According to their research, meaning is not related to your health, financial security, or level of comfort in life, whereas happiness is.

The researchers chose five crucial characteristics to distinguish between a happy life and a meaningful one:

1. Meeting personal needs can make people happy but doesn't necessarily give life meaning.

2. Happiness focuses on the present, while a meaningful life connects the past, present and future.

3. Being social can lead to both happiness and meaning but in different ways. Enjoying time with friends might make us happy while doing something for others gives life a purpose.

4. Challenges, while sometimes stressful, add depth and meaning to life.

5. Expressing oneself can lead to a sense of purpose, even if it doesn't always bring immediate joy.

Even though several studies have found a connection between giving and pleasure, Baumeister claims that this association results from the meaning each individual attaches to giving. One of the more surprising results of the study was that while stealing from others was linked to happiness and not meaning, giving to others was linked to meaning instead of happiness.

Baumeister's work has sparked a discussion about what people and psychologists mean when discussing happiness. His work doubts positive psychology research that relates helpful, pro-social behavior to pleasure and well-being. Baumeister makes it plain that he believes it's important to draw a line between pleasure and purpose, in part to inspire more people to pursue worthwhile endeavors in life regardless of whether doing so makes them feel joyful.

Living a meaningful life enhances happiness, and happiness may also contribute to finding life more meaningful, according to the evidence, he asserted.

Instead of just looking for fun, it might make more sense while trying to live a life well-lived to look for things you find important, such as meaningful connections, selflessness, and self-expression with a purpose, even if enjoying yourself makes one feel more important, according to Baumeister. Chasing happiness without a goal is stressful, uncomfortable, and aggravating.

Since meaning derives from a larger context, you must go outside of yourself to understand the meaning behind what you're doing. There's a good chance that you'll also feel excitement and happiness while travelling. Baumeister advises, "Aim for long-term goals; perform deeds that society values highly—for achievement or moral reasons."

Victor Strecher, a behavioral scientist at the University of Michigan's School of Public Health, lost his daughter, 19, unexpectedly to a heart attack in 2010, and her vulnerability and eventual passing upended his notions about what life should be about and how to live it, which prompted him to write the book *Life on Purpose: How Living for What Matters Most Changes Everything.*

The book discusses how philosophers have long debated the relationship between happiness and meaning and explores the nature of purpose through contemplative and occasionally inspirational stories of people who have found their calling. It includes Strecher's perspectives as well as those of other people who have found their calling and changed the course of their lives.

According to Strecher, psychological well-being and even measures of physical health and lifespan are significantly correlated with your life purpose, which includes trying to live by your beliefs and aspirations and positively impact the world. The book also provides an overview of the recently emerging field of purpose science.

An older person's risk of stroke can be reduced by 22 percent with a one-point difference in purpose, according to studies, and people with heart disease have a 27 percent lower risk of having a heart attack during a two-year period for every one point higher on a six-point scale measuring purpose in life.

The Human Flourishing Program at Harvard University was established in 2016 to explore further the idea of how to flourish as human beings. This could be interpreted to mean that more important than your health is your capacity to overcome challenges, be resilient, and use psychological techniques to handle any situation in life and find fulfillment.

According to Viktor Frankl, finding meaning in our lives directly impacts our mental health, and this is supported by related research, such as that published in the *American Journal of Epidemiology* in 2019 by doctors Ying Chen and Erik Kim. According to this research, having a purpose directly impacts your physical health, psychological balance, self-esteem, and emotional processing. These goals act as an internal support system that lowers loads, so finding meaning in your life also directly impacts these.

What Does It Mean to Be Purposeful?

Being purposeful is more than just setting tangible goals. It's about having a reason to wake up every day, feeling inspired and driven by aspirations, and finding your unique place in the world.

Psychologist Mihaly Csikszentmihalyi, in his book, *Flow: The Psychology of Optimal Experience,* emphasizes that purpose is a force that drives you towards things that are meaningful not just to you, but beyond yourself. Consider wanting to spread happiness within your family or aiding a stranger in need. Your purpose could be writing a book, creating art, or mastering knowledge in a certain field.

Emily Esfahani Smith, in her book *The Power of Meaning: Crafting a Life That Matters,* having a purpose provides people with a sense of direction, resilience in the face of challenges, and a stronger sense of fulfillment.

Studies have also shown a connection between a sense of purpose and favorable health outcomes, including fewer heart attacks and strokes, better sleep, and a decline in dementia and cognitive deficits.

The good news is that you do not have to choose between leading an affluent lifestyle and having a meaningful life. You might find that your sense of purpose affects how much money you make. A 2016 study published in *the Journal of Research and Personality* found that people with a sense of purpose make more money than people who think their work is pointless.

Given all these advantages, it is obvious that discovering your life's importance and purpose is crucial; nonetheless, discovering a person's significance and purpose requires time.

According to a study that was published in *JAMA Psychiatry*, people who felt they had a purpose in life were less likely to have weak grip strength or slow walking speeds, both of which are symptoms of declining physical fitness and disability risk factors. They also noticed that people with a purpose are more committed to taking care of their health.

Obtaining Purpose in Your Life

Consider these inquiries as you begin to define your quest:

- **What injustice, pain, or problem would you truly like to see resolved?** This question can help you figure out what matters to you the most. As soon as you realize this, start developing strategies and objectives for how you will help to resolve this problem. This doesn't have to be a big project. For example, if you truly want to improve the world, you can start by doing random acts of kindness throughout your day.

- **What activities make you feel invigorated and even experience a state of flow where you are so absorbed in what you are doing that you may even lose track of time?** This question can help you further define your life's purpose by allowing you to think about the activities that make you feel invigorated and even experience a flow state.

- ☐ **Do you make sacrifices?** What are the things, people, or causes you are willing to sacrifice? The things that give us meaning in life are often so essential to us that we are willing to sacrifice less significant things like free time or money.

- ☐ **Do you meditate?** Do you use meditation or other forms of introspective practice to help you better understand your beliefs, interests, and experiences?

- ☐ **Have you identified and affirmed your guiding principles?** Have you revisited or reaffirmed your most important values in life, and ensured they are in alignment with your actions and lifestyle.

- ☐ **Are you curious?** If so, use your curiosity to learn more about your passions, interests, and the world in general.

- ☐ **Have you researched the wisdom and experiences of others?** Do you read about, watch and discuss this with others to find inspiration, virtuous behavior and character development?

Good Character and Virtues

People can more successfully navigate life's problems, make informed decisions, and live fulfilling and meaningful lives by emulating virtues and developing a strong positive character. Virtue and good character play a significant part in gaining self-mastery as they serve as the foundation for moral development, personal progress, and general well-being.

I call it the "glue" that holds self-mastery together and refer to it as the strong thread that unites virtues, character, morals, and ethics in my most recent book, *Virtuous Leadership: The Character Secrets of Great Leaders.*

Virtues are ubiquitous and regarded as essential elements of well-being throughout all civilizations. They include moral superiority, goodness, and other wonderful qualities or features.

Character in this book refers to good character, which exhibits moral fortitude, ethical traits, and a variety of attributes. Character can be described as a person's distinctive combination of mental traits and deeds.

Management guru Stephen Covey states, "Our character is essentially a composite of our habits; good character is a show of ethics and morality. Since they are dependable and frequently unconsciously performed routines, they regularly and daily represent our character. "

For instance, leaders like Hitler, Stalin, or Putin would be seen as having dark or "bad" character. In contrast, traits exhibited by leaders like Mandela, Gandhi, or Martin Luther King are seen as having good character.

Positive psychology research has demonstrated that people actively pursuing virtues and character strengths experience greater well-being and flourishing. *The VIA Classification of Strengths,* developed by Christopher Peterson and Martin Seligman, identifies 24 universal character strengths, including kindness, gratitude, perseverance, honesty, and self-regulation.

It's natural to conceive of positive psychology as focusing on stress-free people, but this is wrong, according to Peterson and Seligman. We cannot ignore the bad while emphasizing the good. When discussing character strengths, whether internal or external, we must consider the conditions of difficulties. They list the following characteristics as necessary to do so:

- ☐ Engagement in activities that promote leading a "happy life" for oneself or others.

- ☐ The moral weight they place on their own lives, especially in the absence of favorable results.

- ☐ A show of strength that doesn't make those around them feel inferior.

☐ The absence of an obvious "opposite."

☐ A method that can be evaluated and is at least largely consistent across situations and time.

☐ A unique trait that cannot be replaced by another strength and is drawn from the other strengths that make up the classification system.

☐ "Paragons," or individuals with exceptionally high levels of strength, can display them.

☐ A natural aptitude for it at a young age.

☐ "Institutions and accompanying rituals" that help it expand, implying that at least some elements of society at large purposefully encourage it.

The authors used these criteria to identify characteristics that have been present in societies all over history and the world, each of which has several character strengths connected to exhibiting or practicing the characteristic:

1. **Wisdom and knowledge:** Having convictions, even when they are unpopular; this involves bravery on the physical plane but is not limited to them.

2. **Endurance and perseverance:** finishing what one starts; moving forward despite obstacles; "getting it out the door;" finding satisfaction in accomplishing tasks.

3. **Logic and reasoning:** Using reason before acting.

4. **Honesty:** not making false or exaggerated claims.

5. **Accountability:** Taking ownership of your words and deeds.

6. **Humanity:** The capacity to sympathize with and befriend others.

7. **Love:** cherishing close relationships with people, especially those in which kindness and compassion are shown in return.

8. **Generosity:** (also known as nurturing, caring, compassion, altruistic love, or "niceness").

9. **Justice and citizenship:** Virtues of treating everyone equally and of fostering a strong feeling of community via citizenship.

10. **Forbearance:** humility and modesty.

11. **Transcendence:** Characteristics that give a sense of purpose and connectedness to the universe.

Summary and Follow-Up

A Purpose in Life (PIL) assessment from the Encyclopedia of Quality of Life and Well-Being is included in Appendix D. It is difficult to achieve self-mastery without a strong set of moral and ethical standards to live by. By connecting these standards to a clear understanding of the meaning and purpose of life, you will be better able to act morally when the situation calls for it.

Afterword

Echoes of Wisdom: A Journey Through Time in Self-Mastery

In whispers of time, both ancient and new,
A tale unfolds, a path to pursue.
Self-mastery beckons, a beacon so bright,
A journey internal, a personal flight.

Self-awareness, the key to the gate,
An art mastered by Socrates' fate.
"Know thyself," he declared with insight profound,
In self's reflection, wisdom is found.

With emotion regulation, a stoic's grace,
Epictetus taught, in life's fervent pace,
Not events but our judgment to them we react,
Master feelings and life's course you'll tact.

Empathy blooms, in Buddha's embrace,
A connection to others, a compassionate trace.
A shared human suffering, a kind-hearted view,
Binds us as one, not me versus you.

In compassion's soft glow Confucius we find,
Golden Rule in his words, to others be kind.
Love and understanding, to self-extend too,
Harmony in balance, a moral virtue.

In the bustling world where time slips fast,
Self-mastery's key to make moments last,
Personal productivity, a harmonious art,
A focused mind's tune, a symphonic heart.

Prosocial behavior, a call to act,
In Darwin's notion, a human pact.
Survival not strongest, but those who relate,
Cooperation and kindness determine our fate.

In resilience's embrace, Mandela stood tall,
Facing hardship and strife, transcending the fall.
A will unbroken, a spirit refined,
In perseverance's forge, strength you'll find.

The moral choices we make along the way,
Reflect timeless virtues, in shades of gray.
From Kant to Aristotle, ethics they teach,
A compass internal, it's never out of reach.

In today's spinning world, so fast and so wild,
These elements guide us, adult and child.
A mastery of self, a sacred quest,
In heart, mind and in soul, we find our best.

Modern chaos meets ancient peace,
In self-mastery's garden, our troubles may cease.
From screens and noise, we must turn our eyes,
To inner wisdom that never dies.

Through ages and sages, the message is clear,
Self-mastery's importance is truly sincere.
In knowing oneself, in love and in strife,
Lies the essence, the meaning, the purpose in life.

References

Adderholdt, M. (1999). *Perfectionism: What's Bad About Being Too Good.* New York: Free Spirit Publishing.

Abdullah, S. (2009). *Saffron Dreams.* Ann Arbor MI: Modern History Press.

Aeschylus (1996). *Prometheus Bound.* London, UK: Dover.

Aknin.L.B., et al. (2012). Giving leads to happiness in young children. *PLOS One, 6(5), 26-41.*

Alden, L. E., Wiggins, J. S., & Pincus, A. L. (1990). Construction of circumplex scales for the Inventory of Interpersonal Problems. *Journal of Personality Assessment, 55*(3-4), 521–536.

Aurelius, M.(2006). *Meditations.* New York: Penguin Classics.

Aristotle. (2012). *Nicomachean Ethics.* Chicago: University of Chicago Press.

Baron-Cohen, S. (2011).*The Science of Evil: On Empathy and the Origins of Cruelty. New York: Basic Books.*

Bajaj, B. & Pande, N. (2016). Mediating role of resilience in the impact of mindfulness on life satisfaction and affect as indices of subjective well-being. *Psychological and Cognitive Sciences,*93, 63-67.

Barsade, S.G., & O'Neill, O.A. (2014). A longitudinal study of the culture of companionate love and employee and client outcomes in a long-term care setting. Administrative Science Quarterly, 59(4), 551-598.

Bartlett, M., & DeSteno, D. (2006). Gratitude and prosocial behavior: helping when it costs you. *Psychological Science,* 17(4), 319-325.

Baumister, R.F., et al. (2019). Bad is stronger than good. *Review of General Psychology,* 5 (4), 76-91.

Bazerman, M.H., & Tenbrunsel, A.E. (2012*). Blindspots: Why We Fail to Do What's Right and What to Do About It.* Princeton, NJ: Princeton University Press.

Beenen, G., et al. (2021). The good manager: development and validation of the managerial interpersonal skills scale. *Frontiers of Psychology, 29(12) 631-643.*

Berger, J.G. (2016). *Simple Habits for Complex Times: Powerful Practices for Leaders.* Palo Alto: Stanford Business Books.

Berkowitz, L., & Connor, W. H. (1966). Success, failure, and social responsibility. *Journal of Personality and Social Psychology,* 4(6), 664-669.

Bienvenu, J. (2012) Psychiatric problems in patients who survive illnesses. *Psychiatric Times. Video.*

Bonanno, G. (2019). *The Others Side of Sadness.* New York: Basic Books.

Boyatzis, R., McKee, A. & Goleman, D. (2013). *Primal Leadership: Learning to Lead With Emotional Intelligence.* Cambridge, MA: Harvard Business Review Press.

Bregman, R. (2020). *Humankind: A Hopeful History.* New York: Little, Brown and Company.

Brown, B. (2015). *Rising Strong.* New York: Random House.

Brown, B. (2010). *The Gifts of Imperfection.* New York: Hazelden Publishing.

Brown, S., et al. (2012). Motives for volunteering are associated with mortality risk in older adults. *Health Psychology,* 31(1), 87-96.

Burns, D. (1980). *Feeling Good: The New Mood Therapy*. New York: William Morrow.

Cacioppo, J.T., & Cacioppo, S. (2018). Loneliness in the modern age: an evolutionary theory of loneliness. *Advances in Experimental Psychology*, 58, 127-197.

Caldwell, C., & Hayes, L. (2016). Self-efficacy and self-awareness: moral insights to increased leader effectiveness. *Journal of Management Development*, 35(9), 1163-1173.

Campling, P., & Ballatt, J. (2011). *Intelligent Kindness: Reforming the Culture of Healthcare*. San Francisco: RC Psych Publications.

Cashman, K. (2012). *The Pause Principle: Step Back to Lead Forward*. Oakland, CA. Berrett-Koehler.

Chalmers, W. M. (2010). Training to survive the workplace of today. *Industrial and Commercial Training, 42(5), 36-48.*

Chance, Z. (2022). *Influence is Your Superpower: The Science of Winning Hearts, Sparking Change and Making Good Things Happen*. New York: Random House.

Chen, Y., et al. (2019). Sense of mission and subsequent health and well-being among young adults: an outcome-wide analysis. *American Journal of Epidemiology*, 188(4), 664-673.

Clear, J. (2018). *Atomic Habits*. New York: Avery.

Coetzer, G.H., et al. (2007). Group development and team effectiveness. *The Journal of Applied Behavioral Science*, 43(2).

Connor, M., & Davidson, J.R. (2003). Development of a new resilience scale. *Depression and Anxiety, 18(2), 76-82.*

Covey. S.R. (1989).*The 7 Habits of Highly Effective People*. New York:

Simon & Schuster.

Covington, M. (2007). Self-Esteem, and failure in school: Analysis and policy implications. In: Perry, R.P., Smart, J.C. (eds). *The Scholarship of Teaching and Learning in Higher Education: An Evidence-Based Perspective.* Dordrecht: Springer.

Chowrira, S.G. (2019). DIY productive failure: boosting performance in a large undergraduate biology course. *Science of Learning, 19-40.*

Cox, B. J., Enns, M. W., & Clara, I. P. (2002). The multidimensional structure of perfectionism in clinically distressed and college student samples. *Psychological Assessment,* 14(3), 365–373.

Csikszentmihalyi, M. (2010). *The Man Who Lied to His Laptop: What Machines Teach Us About Human Relationships.* New York: Current.

Cunningham, W., & Kirkland, T. (2011). Neural basis of affect and emotion. *Social Cognitive and Affective Neuroscience,* 2(6), 656-665.

Damasio, A. (2005). *Descartes' Error: Emotion, Reason, and the Human Brain.* New York: Penguin Books.

Damon, W. (2008). *The Path to Purpose: Helping Our Children Find Their Calling in Life.* New York: Free Press.

Daniels. A. (2009). *Oops! 13 Management Practices That Waste Time and Money.* Atlanta, *GA: Performance Management Publications.*

Davis, C., & Cowles, M. (1991). Body image and exercise: A study of relationships and comparisons between physically active men and women. *Sex Roles: A Journal of Research,* 25(1-2), 33–44.

David, S., & Congleton, C. (November 2013). Emotional agility. *Harvard Business Review.*

Davenport, T., & Beck, J.C (2002). *The Attention Economy: Understanding the New Currency of Business.* Cambridge, MA: Harvard

Business Review Press.

De Waal, F. (2010) *The Age of Empathy: Nature's Lessons for a Kinder Society.* New York: Emblem Editions.

DeWall, N., et al. (2011). Tuning in to psychological change: Linguistic markers of psychological traits and emotions over time in popular U.S. song lyrics. *Psychology of Aesthetics, Creativity and the Arts,* 5(3), 200-207.

Dewyze , J. & Mallinger, A. (1993). *Too Perfect: When Being in Control Gets Out of Control.* New York: Ballantine Books.

Diener, E., & Seligman, M.E.P. (2002) Very happy people. *Psychological Science,* 13 (1), 81-84.

Dimoka, A. (2010). Brain mapping of psychological processes with psychometric scales: An fMRI method for social neuroscience. *Neuroimage, 54, 263-271.*

Digksterhuis, M., et al. (2006). On making the right choice: the deliberation-without-attention effect. *Science,* 311(5763), 1005-7.

Drigas, A., & Papoutsi, C. A new layered model on emotional intelligence. *Behavioral Science.* 8(5), 2-17.

Druskat, V. (2005). *Linking Emotional Intelligence and Performance at Work: Current Research Evidence With Individuals and Groups.* New York: Psychology Press.

Duhigg, C. (2014). *The Power of Habit: Why We Do What We Do in Life and Business.* New York: Random House.

Dunn, E., & Norton, M. (2014). *Happy Money: The Science of Happier Spending.* New York: Simon and Schuster.

Duval, S., & Wicklund, R. (1972). *A Theory of Objective Self-Awareness.*

New York Academic Press.

Dweck, C. (2017). *Mindset: Changing The Way You Think To Fulfil Your Potential.* New York: Little, Brown.

Epictetus. (2004). *The Enchiridion.* London, UK: Dover.

Eurich, T. (2018). *Insight: The Surprising Truth About How Others See Us, How We See Ourselves, and Why the Answers Matter More Than We Think.* New York: Currency.

Extremera, N., et al. (2019). The contribution of emotional intelligence to career success: beyond personality traits. *International Journal of Environmental Research and Public Health, 16(23),*4809.

Feldman, R., et al. (2022). Oxytocin reactivity to the therapeutic encounter as a biomarker of change in the treatment of depression. *Journal of Counselling and Psychology,* 69(5), 755-760.

Ferris, T. *(2009). The 4 Hour Workweek* . New York: Harmony.

Flett, G.L., & Hewitt, P.L. (2014). A proposed framework for preventing perfectionism and promoting resilience and mental health among vulnerable children and adolescents. *Psychology in the Schools,* 51(9), 899-912.

Fogg, B.J. (2019). *Tiny Habits: The Small Changes That Change Everything.* Boston: Houghton Mifflin.

Franklin, B. (2007). *Poor Richard's Almanack.* New York: Skyhorse.

Friedman, H.H. & Friedman, L.W. (2018) *Psychosociological Issues in Human Resource* Management. New York: Addleton Academic Publishers.

Frost, R. O., Marten, P., Lahart, C., & Rosenblate, R. (1990). The dimensions of perfectionism. *Cognitive Therapy and Research, 14(5),* 449–468.

Frost, R.O., & Shows, D.L. The nature and measurement of compulsive indecisiveness. *Behavior Research and Therapy*, 3 (7), 683-692.

Frost, P.J. (1999). Why compassion counts. *Journal of Management Inquiry*, 8(2), 127-135.

Fryburg, D., et al. (2020). Kindness media rapidly inspires viewers and increases happiness, calm, gratitude, and generosity in a healthcare setting. *Frontiers of Psychological Science*, 11, 591942.

Gabel, M.S. & McAuley, T. (2022). Why might negative mood help or hinder inhibitory performance? An exploration of thinking styles using a Navon induction. *Cognitive Emotion*, 36(4), 705-712.

Galinsky, A., et al. (2009). "Goals Gone Wild: The Systematic Side Effects of Over-Prescribing Goal Setting. *Harvard Business School Working Paper*.

Germer, C.K., Siegel, R.D., & Fulton, P.R. (2016). *Mindfulness and Psychotherapy*. New York: Guilford Press.

Gentile, D.R. (2012). Nasty people in the media prime the brain for aggression. *Psychology of Popular Media Culture*, 6(3). 212-229.

Gilar-Corbi, R., et al. (2019). Can emotional intelligence be improved? A randomized experimental study of a business-oriented EI training program for senior managers. *PLoS* , 14(10),0224254.

Gilbert, D., & Killingsworth, M. (2010). A wandering mind is an unhappy mind. *Science,* 330(6), 932-945.

Ghuman, P., & Johnson, M. (2020). *Blindsight: The (Mostly) Hidden Ways Marketing Reshapes Our Brains*. Dallas, TX: BenBella Books.

Goleman, D. & Boyatzis, R. (2017). Emotional intelligence has 12 elements. Which do you need to work on? *Harvard Business Review*. February 6.

Gratz, K.L. & Roemer, L. (2004). Multidimensional assessment of emotion regulation and dysregulation: Development, factor structure, and Initial validation of the difficulties in emotion regulation scale. *Journal of Psychopathology and Behavioral Assessment*, 30, 315-326.

Greenspon, T. S. (2000). "Healthy Perfectionism" is an oxymoron! reflections on the psychology of perfectionism and the sociology of science. *Journal of Secondary Gifted Education*, 11, 197-208.

Greenwood, K., & Krol, N. (2020). 8 ways managers can support employees' mental health. *Harvard Business Review*, August 07.

Groysberg, B., & Seligson, S. (2020). Good leaders are an act of kindness. *Working Knowledge*. Harvard Business School.

Haidt, J. (2006). *The Happiness Hypothesis: Finding Modern Truth in Ancient Wisdom.* New York: Basic Books.

Hanson, R. (2009). *Buddha's Brain: The Practical Neuroscience of Happiness, Love and Wisdom.* Oakland, CA: New Harbinger Publications.

Hewlett, S.A. & Luce, C.B. (2008). Stopping the exodus of women in science. *Harvard Business Review*, June.

Hewitt, P. L., Flett, G. L., Sherry, S. B., Habke, M., Parkin, M., Lam, R. W., McMurtry, B., Ediger, E., Fairlie, P., & Stein, M. B. (2003). *Perfectionistic Self-Presentation Scale (PSPS)* [Database record]. *APA PsycTests.*

Hill, P., et al. (2014). Purpose in life as a predictor of mortality across adulthood. *Psychological Science, 25*(7), 1482-1486.

Hobbes, T. (1994). *Leviathan.* London, UK: Hackett Pub. Co.

Hui, B.P.H. (2020). Rewards of kindness? A meta-analysis of the link between prosociality and well-being. *Psychological Bulletin.*, 146(12) 1084-1116.

Isen, A.M. and Daubman, K.A. (1984). The influence of affect on categorization. *Journal of Personality and Social Psychology*, 47, 1206-1217.

Iyengar, S. (2012). *The Art of Choosing.* New York: Twelve Books.

Kahneman, D. (2013). *Thinking, Fast and Slow.* New York: Anchor Books.

Kahneman, D., & Tversky, A. (1979). Prospect Theory: An analysis of decision under risk. *Econometrica*, 47 (2), 263-291.

Klein, G.A. (2017). *Sources of Power: How People Make Decisions.* Boston: MIT Press.

Karnes, R. (2008). A change in business ethics: The impact on employer-employee relations. *Journal of Business Ethics*, 87, 189-197.

Kashdan, T., & Biswas-Diener, R. (2017). *The Upside of Your Dark Side: Why Being Your Whole Self—Not Just Your "Good" Self—Drives Success and Fulfillment.* New York: Avery.

Keltner, D. (2016). *The Power Paradox: How We Gain and Lose Influence.* New York: Penguin Press.

King, L. A., & Burton, C. M. (2003). The hazards of goal pursuit. In E. C. Chang & L. J. Sanna (Eds.), *Virtue, Vice, and Personality: The Complexity of Behavior* (pp. 53–69).

Kraft, H. (2020). *Deep Kindness: A Revolutionary Guide for the Way We Think, Talk, and Act in Kindness.* New York: Simon and Schuster.

Krznaric, R. (2012). *The Wonderbox: Curious Histories of How to Live and How to Find Fulfilling Work.* New York: Profile Books.

Lazarus, R. (1991). *Emotion and Adaptation.* Oxford, UK: Oxford University Press.

Lehrer, J. (2010). *How We Decide.* New York: Houghton Mifflin Harcourt.

Lewis, M. (2016).*The Undoing Project: The Friendship That Changed Our Minds.* New York: WW Norton.

Lieberman, M.D. (2014). *Social: Why Our Brains Are Wired to Connect.* New York: Crown Books.

Lieberman, M.D., & Torre, J.B. (2018). Putting feelings into words: Affect labeling as implicit emotion regulation. *Emotion Review,* 10(2), 116-124.

Lippincott, M. (2018). Deconstructing the relationship between mindfulness and leader effectiveness. *Leadership & Organization Development Journal,* 39(1), 107-125.

Lipton, B. (2016). *The Biology of Belief: Unleashing the Power of Consciousness,* Matter & Miracles. Carlsbad, CA: Hay House.

Lyubomirsky, S., & Layous, K. (2013). How do simple positive activities increase well-being? *Current Directions in Psychological Science,* 22(1), 57-63.

MacCann, C., et al. (2020). Emotional intelligence predicts academic performance: A meta-analysis. *Psychological Bulletin,* 146(2), 150-186.

Mark, G., Iqbal, S., Czerwinski, M., Johns, P., & Sano, A. (2016). Email duration, batching and self-interruption: Patterns of email use on productivity and stress. *Proceedings of the 2016 CHI Conference on Human Factors in Computing Systems.*

Mezirow,J. (1991). *Fostering Critical Reflection in Adulthood: A Guide to Transformative and Emancipatory Learning.* San Francisco, CA: Jossey-Bass.

Mikels, J.A., Maglio, S.J., Reed, A.E., & Kaplowitz. (2011). Should I go with my gut? Investigating the benefits of emotion-focused decision-making. *Emotion, 11(4), 743-53.*

Mikulincer, M., & Shaver, P. (2005). Attachment security, compassion, and altruism. *Current Directions in Psychological Science,* 14, 34-38.

Moser, J. S., Hartwig, R., Moran, T. P., Jendrusina, A. A., & Kross, E. (2014). Neural markers of positive reappraisal and their associations with trait reappraisal and worry. *Journal of Abnormal Psychology, 123(1),* 91–105.

Neff, K. D., Hsieh, Y.-P., & Dejitterat, K. (2005). Self-compassion, Achievement Goals, and Coping with Academic Failure. *Self and Identity,* 4(3), 263–287.

Nass, C., & Yen, C. (2010). *The Man Who Lied to His Laptop: What Machines Teach Us About Human Relationships.* New York: Current.

Nezu, A.M., and Nezu, C.M. (2009). *Problem-Solving Therapy.* New York: Springer.

Nørretranders, T. (1999). *The User Illusion: Cutting Consciousness Down to Size.* New York: Penguin.

Nelson, S.K. et al. (2014). "It's up to you": Experimentally manipulated autonomy support for prosocial behavior improves well-being in two cultures over six weeks. *The Journal of Positive Psychology,* 10(5), 463-476.

Oatley, K., & Johnson-Laird, P.N. (2014). Cognitive approaches to emotions. *Trends in Cognitive Science.,* 18(3), 134-40.

Pearson, J., et al. (2016). Measuring intuition: Nonconscious emotional information boosts decision accuracy and confidence. *Psychological Science,* 27(5), 622-634.

Peck, S. (2003). *The Road Less Travelled: A New Psychology of Love, Traditional Values and Spiritual Growth*. New York: Touchstone.

Pencavel, J. (2015). The productivity of working hours. *The Economic Journal*, 125(589, 2052-2076.

Peterson, C., & Seligman, M. (2004). *Character Strengths and Virtues: A Handbook and Classification*. Cambridge, U.K.: Oxford University Press.

Piff, P.K., et al. (2012). Higher social class predicts increased unethical behavior. *Proceedings of the National Academy of Sciences, 109(11), 4086-4091*.

Plutchik, R. (1958). Outlines of a new theory of emotion. *Transactions of the New York Academy of Sciences, 20, 394–403*.

Posner, M., & Rothbart, M.K.(2000). Developing mechanisms of self-regulation. *Development and Psychopathology*, 12(3), 427-441.

Porter, J. (2019, June) How to move from self-awareness to self-improvement. *Harvard Business Review*.

Poulin, M., Brown. S.L., Dillard, A.J., & Smith, D. (2013). Giving to others and the association between stress and mortality. *American Journal of Public Health*, 103(9), 1649-1655.

Ramachandran, V.S. & Altschuler, E. (2009).The use of visual feedback, in particular mirror visual feedback, in restoring brain functioning. *Brain*, 132, 1693–710.

Rozin, P., & Royzman, E.B. (2001). Negativity bias, negativity dominance, and contagion. *Personality and Social Psychology Review*, 5(4), 296-320.

Rudd, M., Aaker, J., & Norton. M. (2014). Getting the most out of giving: Concretely framing a prosocial goal maximizes happiness. *Journal of Experimental Social Psychology*, 23(10), 1130-6.

Sagi, A., & Hoffman, M. L. (1976). Empathic distress in the newborn. *Developmental Psychology, 12*(2), 175–176.

Sanders, T. (2002). *Love Is the Killer App: How to Win Clients and Win Friends.* New York: Crown.

Sandler, S.A. (2006). *Born Losers: A History of Failure in America.* Cambridge, MA: Harvard University Press.

Schwartz, T. (2011). *The Way We're Working Isn't Working: The Four Forgotten Needs That Energize Great Performance.* New York: Free Press.

Schulz, K. (2011). *Being Wrong: Adventures in the Margin of Error.* New York: Harper Collins.

Seligman, M. (2006). Learned Optimism: How to Change Your Mind and Your Life. New York: Vintage.

Seppälä, E. (2014, June). Why compassion is a better managerial tactic than toughness. *Harvard Business Review.*

Sezer, O., N. K., & Klein, N. (2021). Don't Underestimate the Power of Kindness at Work; Cambridge, MA: Harvard University Press.

Siegel, D.J. (2007). *The Mindful Brain.* New York: WW Norton.

Shaw, R.B. (2004). *Leadership Blindspots: How Successful Leaders Identify and Overcome the Weaknesses That Matter.* San Francisco, CA: Jossey-Bass.

Sitkin, S., et al. (1993). The stretch goal paradox: Audacious targets are widely misunderstood and widely misused. *Harvard Business Review,* 95(1) 2017.

Smith, E.E. (2017).*The Power of Meaning: Crafting a Life That Matters.* New York: Viking.

Steel, P. (2007). The Nature of Procrastination: A Meta-Analytic and Theoretical Review of Quintessential Self-Regulatory Failure. *Psychological Bulletin*, 133, 65-94.

Sterman, J., Yetton, P.W., & Yang, M.M. (2017). Stretch goals and the distribution of organizational performance. *Organization Science*, 28(3), 395-410.

Stoeber, J. (2018). The psychology of perfectionism: An introduction. In J. Stoeber (Ed.), *The Psychology of Perfectionism: Theory, Research, Applications* (pp. 3–16). New York: Routledge/Taylor & Francis Group.

Strecher, A. (2016). *Life on Purpose: How Living for What Matters Most Changes Everything*. New York: HarperOne.

Sutton, A. (2016). Measuring the effects of self-awareness: Construction of the self-awareness outcomes questionnaire. *Europe's Journal of Psychology*, 12(4), 645-658.

Telle, N. (2015). Positive empathy and prosocial behavior: A neglected link. *Emotion Review*, 8(2),154-163.

Tolle, E. (2004). *The Power of Now: A Guide to Spiritual Enlightenment*. Novato, CA: New World Library.

Twenge, J.M., & Campbell, W. K. (2010). *The Narcissism Epidemic: Living in the Age of Entitlement*. New York: Atria.

Ulber, J., & Tomasello, M. (2020). Young children's prosocial responses toward peers and adults in two social contexts. *Journal of Experimental Child Psychology*, 198, 104888.

Vanderkam, L. (2012). *What Most Successful People Do on the Weekend*. New York: Portolio.

Wanzer, M.B., & Booth-Butterfield, M. (2018). Humor stress and coping. *Current Issues in Work and Organizational Psychology*, 10, 51-56.

Wegner, D., Schneider, D.J., Carter, S.R., and White, T.L. (1987). Paradoxical effects of thought suppression. found that suppressing feelings and thoughts can have negative effects. *Journal of Personality and Social Psychology*, 53 (1), 22-29.

Williams, R., & Fannin, J.L. (2022). Leading-edge neuroscience reveals significant correlations between beliefs, the whole-brain state, and psychotherapy. *CAPA Quarterly, August.*

Zaki, J. (2019). *The War for Kindness: Building Empathy in a Fractured World.* New York: Crown.

Zaltman, G. (2003). *How Customers Think: Essential Insights into the Mind of the Market.* Cambridge, MA: Harvard University Press.

Appendix A

Strategies for Attaining Self-Mastery

Here are some ways in which leaders (and the public also) can enhance and develop their self-awareness and self-reflection. To complete a Self-Awareness Assessment, see Appendix B.

Set aside regular and structured time for self-reflection (daily or weekly). "Calendarize" it just as you would a meeting or appointment. Some self-aware executives I know do this on a Monday morning or on Sunday evening to set up a positive mindset for the week.

Become the observer of your mind through mindfulness meditation. Keep your attention focused on your breath. If you notice your mind wandering to other thoughts, gently return your attention to your breath.

Learn to recognize "cognitive distortions" and biases. These are inaccurate thoughts and beliefs that warp how we see things, including ourselves, and biases that affect our beliefs. Examples are confirmation bias, catastrophizing, and blaming. Catch yourself when you notice you've lapsed into that kind of thinking.

Keep a journal. The more you journal, the more you are aware of your behaviors and thought patterns, and subsequently, the more able you become to change and grow. Writing helps us process our thoughts and makes us feel connected and at peace with ourselves. Research shows that recording things we are grateful for, or our challenges helps increase happiness and satisfaction.

Travel and learn about other cultures to gain different perspectives. Spending all your time with your "tribe," geographic location or cultural influences can increasingly narrow your perspective. Find out how other people see things so you can reflect on your perceptions.

Conduct a cognitive reappraisal. This psychological strategy can be understood in the question, *Is the glass half empty or half full?* Cognitive reappraisal is reinterpreting or reframing a negative event to reduce the negative response or completely replace it with a positive one.

Turn off your autopilot. Identify one of your automatic behaviors or habits that you are unhappy about or would like to change and commit to changing them.

State or reaffirm your values. Write down your most important values and ideals associated with your personal life and work, and imagine ways to ensure they align with your behaviors.

State, clarify and reaffirm your core beliefs and how they relate to your identity. What we believe about ourselves, others, and the world help to shape our identity and how we present that identity to the world.

Recognize and deal with your inner conflicts. Resolve any beliefs, values, or emotions that you may have that conflict with each other.

Read high quality fiction. The very best writers are expert observers of human nature. It's their job to notice the tiny details of thought, emotion, desire, and action that most of us miss amid the frantic business of daily life. And even though most of us probably aren't called to be authors and astute observers of human nature professionally, we can all learn a thing or two about ourselves by learning to pay attention like an author. By describing people carefully, good fiction teaches us to think about people carefully and compassionately. And the better we get at observing others, the more likely we are to look at ourselves the same way.

Do a self-awareness assessment. Completing a self-awareness assessment allows you to reflect and review the degree to which you may be self-aware and consider steps to expand that awareness.

Ask yourself some self-awareness questions and write your answers in a journal. Periodically review them.

Work with a formal mentor, coach, or counsellor. They can provide skillful feedback and issues for self-examination that will assist you greatly toward self-mastery.

Draw a timeline of your life. Spend 20 minutes drawing a timeline of your life, starting with your birth, and mark the major events along the timeline. Specifically, note events that impacted you--big or small, positive or negative. This helps you to make sense of or get a new perspective on an especially distressing or difficult time by seeing that specific period "in context."

Ask for feedback from others (and take it well), independent of any formal assessment. Most people don't deliberately seek feedback about themselves from others unless it's because of a process at work. There are many aspects of ourselves that we can see need improvement, it's the parts of ourselves we can't see--our blind spots--that are the real problem. And other people are uniquely positioned to notice these and help us see them.

Be a better listener and observer. Practice being a better listener for others, by consistently practicing your active listening skills. This can include restraining your impulse to think about your response while they are speaking. Good listening should not only involve your cognitive processes, but also something called "empathetic listening," which is noticing the speaker's feelings and emotions. Finally, spend less time speaking, and more time listening (70-30 is good), which facilitates your ability to notice more about what's going on.

Allocate "do nothing" time in your schedule. Research has shown that regular periods of time in which you are not engaging in "doing" or tasks enhances your productivity, well-being, and creativity.

Be rigorous about screening distractions in your life. Constantly being interrupted by a cellphone, email, TV, or meetings has been shown to impact our cognitive performance and increase stress negatively. Also, most of these distractions are in the "external" world, and have no connection to our inner state, and therefore can mask, not enhance, our self-awareness.

Regularly seek out time for solitude, silence and stillness. This engages your mind in a different, creative, and productive way, allowing you to reflect without interruptions or be engaged in activities. It also has been proven to enhance physical well-being.

Learn and regularly practice mindfulness meditation. This activity has aided cognitive focus and attention and enhanced non-judgment, acceptance, and compassion.

Recognize your "inner parents." How are you a reflection of your parents? The influence of our parents is pervasive. Beliefs, values, behaviors, and personal paradigms are all heavily influenced by our parents. How are you carrying your parental influence?

Reflect and act on how you may engage in self-sabotage. Getting in our own way or creating our own obstacles can prevent you from fully engaging in self-awareness. Do you know how you sabotage your efforts or behaviors? Are you blaming others instead of looking inwards? What are you doing about it?

Appendix B

A Self-Awareness Self-Assessment

1. When you make a mistake, it doesn't disrupt your day.

2. You accept the fact that you were not as good at something as you thought you were.

3. You cope with situations that force you to see yourself in a different way.

4. You don't wish to receive praise from others frequently.

5. You don't compare your standards to those of others.

6. You don't frequently criticize your own work.

7. You don't feel guilty when you have not performed to standards.

8. You don't frequently question your abilities.

9. You don't agonize over your performance after a failure.

10. You don't compare your performance to the performance of others.

11. You understand how your characteristics and experiences have led you to become who you are today.

12. You understand how your personal characteristics lead to your behavior in different situations.

13. You use diverse perspectives to arrive at new conclusions about yourself.

14. Your friends describe you as someone who knows themselves well.

15. After a major accomplishment, how likely are you to sit back and

enjoy the moment?

16. You know what qualities you bring to a relationship.

17. You consciously think about the ways your thoughts and emotions influence your behavior.

18. Your friends describe you as sometimes introspective.

19. You spend time alone so you could have time to think.

20. How often do you enjoy time alone because it allows you to reflect on your day's activities?

21. You set time aside to reflect on your day.

22. You ponder over how to improve yourself from knowledge of previous experiences.

23. You integrate information about yourself from different sources to better understand yourself.

24. You often find yourself searching internally for explanations of your behavior and emotions.

25. You frequently have the outcomes of your behavior in each situation that caused you to reach an "a-ha" moment about yourself.

26. You spend time trying to understand yourself

27. You spend thinking about the reasons for your behaviors?

If you responded positively (indicating agreement) to most questions, your self-awareness is well-developed.

Appendix C

Strategies for Managing Your Thoughts and Emotions

1. **Mindfulness meditation.** This involves focusing on the present moment, acknowledging and accepting your thoughts and emotions without judgment. It can help cultivate self-awareness and reduce emotional reactivity, as the research by Jon Kabat-Zinn and B.K. Holzel has shown.

2. **Cognitive restructuring.** This strategy involves identifying and challenging negative or irrational thoughts and replacing them with more realistic and positive ones. According to renowned researchers David Burns and Aaron Beck, you can influence your emotional responses by changing your thinking patterns.

3. **Emotion regulation techniques.** According to M.M. Linehan and J.J. Gross, this strategy involves recognizing and managing your emotions effectively through techniques such as deep breathing exercises, physical activities, self-care, and seeking social support.

4. **Journaling.** Writing down your thoughts and emotions in a journal can provide an outlet for self-expression and reflection. It lets you gain insight into your feelings and experiences and identify patterns or triggers.

5. **Practicing emotional acceptance.** This is the ability to experience your emotions without judgment or having secondary thoughts or emotions about your initial emotion. You just let your emotions be as they are, and they will eventually spontaneously dissipate on their own.

6. **Being more flexible and adaptable.** A lack of emotional regulation lowers your ability to adapt to life changes. You become more

prone to distractions and fail our coping mechanisms. Becoming more flexible and adaptable to situations strengthens your ability to manage emotions.

7. **Practicing self-compassion.** Reminding yourself of your talents and virtues and engaging in less self-critical self-talk help build emotion regulation skills.

8. **Monitoring and changing your self-talk.** Pay attention to the narrative in your head and the voice inside your head. Challenge and change the negative self-talk.

9. **Knowing your triggers.** To master emotion regulation, one must be aware of what triggers them. Triggers are of various kinds. Be aware of the triggers by your physical signs such as shortness of breath, tightened muscles, anger and irritability, the urge to do something impulsive or uncontrollable thoughts.

10. **Using third-person self-talk,** Refer to yourself by your own name. This provides the necessary psychological distance between the self and the emotion-inducing reactions.

11. **Physical distancing.** This skill involves looking at your situation as a "fly on the wall," as though through the eyes of another instead of yourself.

12. **Temporal distancing.** This strategy involves thinking about the situation causing the emotional reaction from the perspective of the future, rather than the present. How would you view it a week from now? A month? A year? Five years? Ten?

Appendix D

A Life Purpose/Meaning Assessment

A 20-item evaluation tool, the PIL (Purpose in Life) Test was created by Gena Davies, Derrick Klaassen, and Alfried Langle and published in the *Encyclopedia of Quality of Life and Well-Being* Research. You respond to its inquiries using a Likert scale with a range of 1 to 7 (in descending order).

The assessment examines:

☐ Meaning perception. This gauges how much importance a person spends on life. It tries to gauge how firmly people believe that there are good reasons to live.

☐ Understanding of the meaning. This gauges whether the subject believes life to be a positive experience.

☐ Tasks and goals. Here, the evaluation probes the subject's objectives and sense of ownership over them.

☐ The discussion of freedom and fate. This element investigates the test belief-takers that death is an uncontrollable force that people should be afraid of.

PIL test questions 1 through 10

1. My usual range is from 1 (totally bored) to 7. (enthusiastic).

2. Life always appears to me to be: 1 (totally routine) to 7 (always exciting).

3. I have between 1 (no purpose or desire) and 7 in my life (many well-defined goals and desires).

4. The scale of my existence ranges from 1 (meaningless) to 7 (full of meaning and purpose).

5. From 1 (which is the same every day) through 7 (always new and different).

6. If I had the option, I would pick from 1 (never to have been born) through 7. (to have nine more lives just like this one)

7. I'll do anything from 1 (laze around for the rest of my life) to 7 (do the thrilling things I've always wanted to do) after I retire.

8. In terms of achieving my life goals, I've gone from 1 (haven't advanced) to 7 (have achieved all of them completely).

9. My life ranges from 1 (empty and desperate) to 7 (a collection of good and exciting things).

10. If I were to pass away right now, I would say that my life has been from 1 (total garbage) to 7 (very valuable).

PIL test questions 11 through 20

11. When I consider my own life: 1 (I frequently wonder myself, "Why am I here? ") to 7 (I always find reasons to live).

12. In terms of my own life, the world ranges from 1 (which baffles me) to 7 (which significantly adapts to my life).

13. My self-assessment ranges from 1 (an irresponsible person) to 7 (a very responsible person).

14. In terms of the freedom people must make their own decisions, I think that people range from 1 (total slaves of the constraints of their natural habitats and situations) to 7 (fully free) (free to make all their life choices).

15. In terms of death, I range from 1 (terrified and prepared) to 7 (prepared and unafraid of it).

16. In terms of suicide, the range is from 1 (I've seriously considered it as a way out of my circumstance) to 7 (I've never given it a second consideration).

17. My ability to discover a sense of direction and meaning in life, in my opinion, ranges from 1 (almost nonexistent) to 7. (Very great).

18. I have no control over my life, and external events dictate everything from 1 to 7. (In my hands and under my control).

19. Dealing with my everyday activities ranges from 1—a tedious and painful experience—to 7 (a source of pleasure and satisfaction).

20. I've learned that: from 1 (I have no life's purpose or mission) to 7 (clear goals and a satisfactory purpose for my life).

Interpretation of the PIL Test Scores

Remember that the maximum score you can receive on this assessment is 140. People who receive scores below 90 may be drifting aimlessly through life. On the other hand, people who score between 90 and 105 points do have a purpose in life, although a vague one. Finally, according to the test's developer, people who score higher than 105 have distinct goals and a strong sense of purpose in life.

Everyone finds meaning in life in a different and personal way. Additionally, it evolves during a person's life. It is your responsibility to find that source of inspiration that will drive them throughout the day.

About the Author

Ray Williams has provided executive coaching, speaking and professional consulting services worldwide. He has over 40 years of experience as a Superintendent of Schools, CEO, senior HR executive, management consultant, trainer, executive coach, hypnotherapist, professional speaker, and author. He has received his undergraduate and graduate training in History, English, Organizational Psychology and Leadership. He is a Certified Master Executive Coach and Certified Hypnotherapist.

He is currently retired as President and CEO of Ray Williams Associates, an executive coaching firm based in Vancouver, providing coaching, and mentoring to executives in the public and private sectors worldwide. He also was an associate of ViRTUS Inc., a leadership development company based in Vancouver.

Ray has recently worked as a consultant for the Holisec Group, which has created the first personality-based coaching app called TheGoodlife.ai.

He is past president of the International Coach Federation in Vancouver and held several board positions professional associations in North America. In addition, he has served as a director and Vice-Chair for the Vancouver Board of Trade and director for several community organizations.

His clients have included Fortune 500 companies, the Best Managed Companies in Canada, and dozens of small businesses and entrepreneurial start-ups. He has been recognized as one of the top C-Suite coaches in Canada.

He has written extensively about leadership, the workplace, organizations, personal development, and social issues including four books on leadership; contributed to several books organizational issues; a novel and screenplay; and been interviewed or written articles for national publications and the media such as *The National Post, The Financial Post, The*

Washington Post, Entrepreneur, The Globe and Mail, the Vancouver Sun, USA Today and Inc., and online media such as Psychology Today, Medium and Sivana East.

His previous books are:

The Leadership Edge: Strategies to Transform School Systems.

Eye of the Storm: How Mindful Leaders Can Transform Chaotic Workplaces.

Toxic Bosses: Practical Wisdom for Developing Wise, Ethical and Moral Leaders.

Macho Men: How Toxic Masculinity Harms Us All and What To Do About It.

I Know Myself and Neither Do You: Why Charisma, Confidence and Pedigree Won't Take You Where You Want to Go.

Virtuous Leadership: The Character Secrets of Great Leaders.

And he has been a contributing author to the following books:

☐ Ready, Aim, Influence!

☐ Systemic Change: Touchstones for the Future School.

Beyond his professional training and experience, he brings his insights into human behavior, having been born and raised in Hong Kong, where his family was imprisoned for four years by the Japanese in WWII, which allows him a unique perspective on resilience, overcoming adversity and sustaining a positive outlook.

Praise for *The Journey to Self-Mastery*

"*The Journey to Self-Mastery* is a profound guide to personal growth and self-discovery. In a landscape crowded with self-development literature, where generic advice often drowns out meaningful insights and actionable strategies, this book shines as a beacon of wisdom. Ray's insights into self-awareness, emotional intelligence, resilience, and moral choices provide valuable tools for navigating life's complexities. Whether you're seeking personal transformation or looking to enhance your leadership skills, this book is an invaluable resource." -- **Dr. Marshall Goldsmith**, the *Thinkers50* #1 Executive Coach and *New York Times* bestselling author of *The Earned Life*, *Triggers*, and *What Got You Here Won't Get You There*.

"Ray Williams' latest book, *The Journey to Self-Mastery*, explores with great insight the importance of mastering our internal lives as the road to finding true personal improvement, fulfillment and transformation. The focus on self-mastery is a timely perspective in a sometimes chaotic and frantic world. The book is anchored in research and rich with concrete strategies and ideas that can benefit anyone wishing to find calmness, purpose and the 'true north' in their lives. *The Journey to Self-Mastery* is an invaluable resource for everyone, and I highly recommend it."--**Emma Seppälä, Ph.D.**, Psychologist, International Keynote Speaker, Science Director, Stanford University Center for Compassion and Altruism Research and Education; Faculty Director of the Yale School of Management's Women's Leadership Program, and best-selling author of *The Happiness Track*.

"Self-mastery takes hard work. Fortunately, Ray Williams has made it just a bit easier with his newest book, *The Journey to Self-Mastery*. Williams, an executive coach and best-selling author, provides a roadmap for learning about yourself and how to become more focused on personal development to enable you to serve others more effectively. Also included are exercises that readers can access to help them learn as they go. Of note are chapters on compassion and moral choices, very valuable and necessary for navigating our world today." -- **John Baldoni,** a member of Marshall Goldsmith's 100 Coaches; 2022 Global Gurus Top 20; Inc.com Top 50; Master Corporate Executive Coach, and the author of many books on leadership, including *Grace Under Pressure: Leading Through Change and Crisis.*

Ray Williams' new book, *The Journey to Self-Mastery: Unlocking the Secrets to Personal Transformation,* is timely and essential. Williams persuasively argues that the true path to personal improvement and life fulfillment lies within us, not in the external world. He clearly analyzes and describes the elements of self-mastery, backed by research, and provides the reader with concrete strategies and tips for self-mastery. In today's world of chaos and conflict, *The Journey to Self-Mastery* is a must-read for anyone seeking personal growth and calm purpose. I highly recommend this book." —**Professor M.S. Rao, Ph.D.,** The Father of "Soft Leadership" and International Leadership Guru.

"This very important book sums up what few know to be important on the road to a successfu happy life. Mastering your mind, thoughts, and emotions unlocks a wea ᶜ success that you will not find elsewhere - not at home, work or throug̣ ᵔnships. Instead of seeking external success, Ray encourages you to ge̩ ̦o within, reflect, adjust, and find your own North Star on the journey. Read and act on his wisdom. You'll be glad you did."-- **Stephanie Frank,** Co-Founder of TheGoodLife.ai, CEO of the Holosec Group, and Author of the best-seller, *The Accidental Millionaire.*

"Leader success in the corporate world is often seen as being able to master external things such as goals, planning, and execution, but my experience in training and working with leaders is mastery of oneself is the key to enduring success. *The Journey to Self-Mastery* is a valuable guide for aspiring and current leaders desiring to follow that journey to self-mastery, and ultimately personal transformation."-- **Bing Chen,** President & CEO, Atlas Corp. (Seaspan Corporation and APR Energy Limited).

Ray Williams has written another great book. *The Journey to Self-Mastery: Unlocking the Secrets to Personal Transformation* is a welcome addition to his series of books, which are valuable resources for people